"*This Present Paradise* is an invitation into the secret garden of prayer, where we can find the truest desire of our hearts—union with God. I was captivated by the prophetic life of St. Elizabeth of the Trinity and found myself longing to dive deeper into the heart of the Trinity. With the perfect balance of spiritual inspiration and practical wisdom, this book will meet you wherever you are in your spiritual journey and take you deeper."

—Michelle Benzinger
Host, *Abiding Together* Podcast,
Creative Director, Greenhouse Collective

"Thirty years ago, I was introduced to and deeply touched by the life and writings of St. Elizabeth of the Trinity. Now, Claire Dwyer has written an excellent, relevant book that dynamically brings to life the saint and her wisdom. The author skillfully leads the reader to the depths of St. Elizabeth's feminine genius, thereby presenting the irresistible beauty of authentic holiness. I found myself not wanting to put the book down because of its engaging style. I highly recommend this book for Catholics who desire friendship with a saint who offers a treasury for our present generation. May this book be spread far and wide because its contents are transformative and timeless."

—Kathleen Beckman
Author, *A Family Guide to Spiritual Warfare*
and *Praying for Priests*

"The desire for home is built into all of us, but it never ends with four walls. Our longing, whether we know it or not, is to dwell with God in our own hearts. St. Elizabeth of the Trinity is a little-known saint, but her genius was to describe this mystery of the interior life. In *This Present Paradise*, Claire Dwyer acquaints us with this remarkable woman and allows the saint to open the doors of our hearts to the unfathomable grace offered to each of us through an authentic relationship with God."

—Carrie Gress
Author, *Theology of Home*

T0025796

"For the everyday busy woman, Claire Dwyer's book is a wonderful devotional to help you deepen your spirituality and find peace in this uncertain time. It's practical, easy, and for women of all ages!"

—Crystalina Evert
Author, speaker, founder of Women Made New

"God calls us to Him through the small, seemingly insignificant moments of our lives. Through beautiful reflections and her own story, Claire draws us deep into the heart of St. Elizabeth and the Heart of the Blessed Trinity. Don't miss this remarkable prayer through story."

—Stephanie Burke
Executive Director, Avila Foundation

"I had never heard of St. Elizabeth of the Trinity, but I can think of no more delightful way to be introduced to her than through the words of Claire Dwyer. Dwyer is a gifted storyteller who seamlessly weaves together scenes from her own life with the life of this beautiful young saint. This book is a biographical and spiritual journey that will leave you inspired and encouraged on your own path toward Heaven."

—Danielle Bean
Author, speaker, and manager of CatholicMom.com

"I'm tremendously grateful to Claire Dwyer for introducing me in such a profound fashion to the life and teachings of St. Elizabeth of the Trinity. Much more than a biography, *This Present Paradise* invites the reader into a beautiful retreat as Dwyer weaves personal vignettes with stories of St. Elizabeth's journey. Eminently engaging, Dwyer's work here will impact many souls!"

—Lisa M. Hendey
Author, *I'm a Saint in the Making*

"St. Elizabeth of the Trinity is a gentle friend with a mighty voice, and Claire's introduction reveals a saint whose special wisdom you didn't know you needed."

—Sonja Corbitt
Bible Study Evangelista

"*This Present Paradise* is a beautiful guide into the profound life of St. Elizabeth of the Trinity and shares just how much she has to offer us in our daily lives. The depth of spirituality and truth in this book is a well from which I will draw again and again. The Lord truly wove a beautiful story in St. Elizabeth's life, and it leads me to a desire of longing in my own prayer life. The book is a sure A+ for spiritual reading: it has increased my desire to know more about Our Heavenly Father through prayer."

—Jenna Guizar
Founder and Creative Director, Blessed Is She

"Claire Dwyer's writing is exquisite. In *This Present Paradise*, she weaves her own story with that of St. Elizabeth of the Trinity. With St. Elizabeth as her guide, Claire explores the reality that there is a sacred space in each of our souls that is designed by the Holy Spirit, where we can hold constant vigil, even in the midst of the noise and chaos of the outside world. When we feel anxious or scared, we must remember that God is there to remind us time and again that we are loved."

—Terry Polakovic
Co-Founder of Endow
Author, *Life and Love: Opening Your Heart to God's Design*
and *Women of Hope*

"How do we embrace the communion of saints? We invite them to join us on our spiritual journeys as dear friends and guides. Claire Dwyer introduces St. Elizabeth of the Trinity to us in *This Present Paradise*, blending her insights into her vocation with St. Elizabeth's reflections as a Carmelite. Beautifully written."

—Kimberly Hahn
Author, apologist, founder of Beloved and Blessed

This Present Paradise

Elizabeth of the Trinity (born Elizabeth Catez),
at the age of twenty.

Claire Dwyer

This Present Paradise
A Spiritual Journey
with St. Elizabeth of the Trinity

SOPHIA INSTITUTE PRESS

Manchester, New Hampshire

Sophia Institute Press
Box 5284, Manchester, NH 03108
1-800-888-9344

www.SophiaInstitute.com

Sophia Institute Press® is a registered trademark of Sophia Institute.

paperback ISBN 978-1-64413-287-6

ebook ISBN 978-1-64413-288-3

Library of Congress Control Number: 2020946010

Fourth printing

For Delaney,
Joseph,
John Paul,
Mary Grace,
Daniel,
Gemma,
and
Justin:
There's no one I'd rather spend
this present paradise with.

Contents

Foreword

God calls forth every human person into existence. From the moment you entered your mother's womb, the Lord infused your soul with an insatiable desire to know Him. In His infinite love, He provides all you need to fulfill that desire — and not just as a mere knowing of facts, but in the sense of a *divine knowing*, an inexpressible intimacy with God in the very depths of your being.

Jesus came to reconcile all of us into the loving arms of the Father and then to release the Holy Spirit to draw us ever more deeply into the heart of the Blessed Trinity. It is in this deepest chasm of love, in the center of the Trinity, that we come to that divine knowing.

If that were not enough, He then poured Himself into the hearts of His saints and through them, radiated powerful light and clarity on the pathway to intimacy and union with Him. One of the most powerful saints who guide us in this journey is Elizabeth of the Trinity, who stands among other towering guides, such as Teresa of Avila, John of the Cross, and Thérèse of Lisieux.

In our time, there are those who write about the saints and those who know them. Claire Dwyer strikes me as one who lives in both realities. In this case, she reveals the depth and beauty of

This Present Paradise

St. Elizabeth's wisdom to help us meet God in the present moment — the only place we can meet Him in this life.

I offer one piece of advice to you as you explore the depths and riches of this book: if you want to know Elizabeth of the Trinity and the God whom she knows, don't read this book quickly. Read it slowly. Read it out loud. If you can, without disturbing others, read it out loud in adoration. Regardless, if you read it with attention and devotion, you will come to know Elizabeth and she will no doubt lead you to her deepest love and desire. She will show you the way and help you understand that "to be happy with Him forever in the next world can begin right now, in this one" — in *this present paradise*.

—Dan Burke
Founder of the Avila Institute for Spiritual Formation
Feast of St. Elizabeth of the Trinity, November 8, 2020

Introduction

My desk was littered with books, articles, scribbled notes—and the glaring whiteness of a blank computer screen, with a blinking cursor reminding me in a steady silent beat: *You - have - nothing. You - have - nothing. You - have - nothing.*

I had no idea where to start. This saint had taken me on long ago (a wise priest once assured me that we don't choose our saints: they choose us), and I was letting her down. I wanted to capture some of her wisdom, to frame it in a fresh way, to introduce her to other modern mothers who needed to know that a young Carmelite, in a supreme act of love over a century ago, had written a retreat for someone just like them.

St. Elizabeth of the Trinity, a Carmelite nun from Dijon, France, wrote a luminous retreat—a series of reflections to be read over ten days—for her married sister, Guite, as a sort of last testament just months before she died in 1906 at the age of twenty-six.

At the time, Elizabeth's younger sister was a mother at home with two young children and all wrapped up, like so many of us, in the cares of life. She couldn't count on the confines of a Carmel to ensure hours of silent prayer and spiritual reading. *No matter,* teaches Elizabeth. *You can have a cloistered heart.*

1

Decades before Vatican II called for the sanctification of the laity, Elizabeth prophetically illustrated that holiness is just as much for the layperson—yes, even the mother at home—as for the religious. Every woman can discover the sanctuary in her soul. She can worship day and night in the sacred silence of her inner temple with her God, who waits for her there. In one of her last letters to Guite, Elizabeth affectionately offers to pray for her little nieces, that they "might always walk in the bright splendor of God and be contemplatives like their little mama."[1]

She had learned this lesson herself as she waited longingly to enter the convent, pining for a life devoted to God but held back by her mother's hesitation. And then, in that place of waiting, God had reminded her that He is not confined to the convent. In a poem for Pentecost two years before she entered Carmel, Elizabeth wrote that her vocation was not 'Carmel' but 'union.' And this vocation can be lived anywhere. In the delay, God had allowed her—no doubt, in part for our sakes a century later—to see that her hope was "founded in Jesus alone/ And while living in the midst of the world/ May I breathe Him alone, see Him alone/ Him my love, my divine Friend!"[2]

I remember exactly where I was standing in the backyard, holding a book of her writings when I realized that I had found a saint who perfectly bridged the divide between the Carmel and the kitchen, the chasm separating the cloister and the carpool.

But now, *I - had - nothing.*

[1] Letter 311 in *I Have Found God, Complete Works*, vol. 2, *Letters from Carmel*, trans. Anne Englund Nash (Washington, DC: ICS Publications, 2014), 328.

[2] St. Elizabeth of the Trinity, "Pentecost," in *Elizabeth of the Trinity: The Unfolding of Her Message*, by Joanne Mosley, vol. I, *In the World and in the Community* (Oxford: Teresian Press, 2012), 59.

Introduction

I didn't know how to do this gem of heaven any justice. Surrounded by other people's words and wisdom, I felt my own inadequacy as I had never felt it before. And then, just like that, she gave me the answer.

My eyes fell on one of her first letters to Guite after she had left home for the convent. Gently she wrote, "I would advise you to simplify all your reading, to fill yourself a little less, you will see that this is much better. Take your Crucifix, look, listen."[3]

Oh, Elizabeth, you were telling me that the starting point was not in a commentary, no matter how brilliant. It was not in a biography, no matter how complete. It was not in a compilation of letters or pages of poems. It was not in your words at all, or in your life, or in your legacy.

It was in Him.

If the end was union with God, then so must I begin. To understand Elizabeth, I needed to be reintroduced to the One she loved so well. Here I would find the starting point, the ending point, the center point.

Fittingly, it was in the midst of the Pentecost novena that I had found myself hunched over books and papers. I shoved everything aside and sat for a moment, finally still. With my eyes on the crucifix suspended on the wall next to me, I smiled.

Yes, Elizabeth. You are right. *I have everything.*

---

[3] Letter 93, in Nash, *Complete Works*, vol. 2, 23.

1

A Threefold Cord

I was self-conscious as my dad led me through the hospital lobby, my First Communion veil blowing behind me. I wore the white dress that day for Grandma, who wouldn't be at the church. The cancer was consuming her, and she didn't have long to live.

It was so hard for her to turn her head as I tiptoed to the bedside, but Grandma managed a faint smile for me. I was shocked at how gaunt she was, how frail. Her life was slipping away. This was the first time death would touch me; I was seven years old. Just a few weeks later, I was with my mom when my dad called, and she held me as she choked out the news of Grandma's death. When Dad returned home, he seemed empty. It was the first time I saw my father cry.

A few months later, my dad's dad was gone, too. Suddenly, unexpectedly, this time — a heart attack. I was in the room when Dad got the call from his brother, and my own heart stopped as I watched him run out of the house that summer day.

For weeks afterward, the sound of the phone would put me into a panic. I would flee into the basement whenever it rang. Sitting on the steps, my hands over my ears, I rocked back and forth and prayed. *Please, God. Please don't let anybody else die.*

This Present Paradise

Death changes a child. Things that seemed stable and safe suddenly shift like sand beneath a receding wave. St. Elizabeth of the Trinity would know loss early and in a very intimate way, and it would change her life, as it does for all of us.

She was born on July 18, 1880, the first child of Joseph Catez, a French military captain, and Marie Rolland. They were a devout and loving couple, and three years later, they welcomed another daughter, Marguerite, known as "Guite."

Elizabeth wasn't even two years old when her mother's mother died and her grandfather came to live with the family. By the time she was five, both her father and her grandfather had retired, and they spent many happy hours at home with Elizabeth and Guite. To have their father's and grandfather's affectionate and undivided attention must have delighted the little girls. But the family circle would contract suddenly, devastating them all: Elizabeth's grandfather would die, and then, within a year, her father would die of a heart attack.

Elizabeth was only seven when she watched her father die that Sunday morning. "I tried to hold back / That last, so very long sigh,"[4] she wrote years later.

He had held her all her short life; now she beheld him as he left this world. I can't imagine what that would do to a little girl, to be so young and so close to the shattering reality of death. "In a sense," the *Catechism of the Catholic Church* says, "bodily death is natural, but for faith it is in fact 'the wages of sin.'" (CCC 1006; Rom. 6:23; cf. Gen. 2:17). In other words, we reel from separation because we were never created for it. "Even though man's nature is mortal, God had destined him not to die" (CCC 1008). Elizabeth's life, however, would become more and more a vivid illustration

---

[4]   St. Elizabeth of the Trinity, Poem 37, in Mosley, *Elizabeth of the Trinity*, vol. 1, 7.

of Christian hope—that our death brings to completion what Baptism begins: our participation in not only the death but also the Resurrection of Jesus Christ.

Hope rises in time
from all places subject to death—
hope is its counterweight.
The dying world unveils its life again
in hope.[5]

—Pope St. John Paul II

After this traumatic event, Elizabeth's mother, Madame Catez, moved her two daughters to a smaller flat on the other side of town, where Elizabeth's room overlooked the garden of the nearby Carmelite convent. Something new—and hopeful—stirred within her as she gazed beyond the walls into that mysterious, prayerful world below.

That something would eventually sever the tight trio of her small family, but this time it would be a slow cut. Her mother, now alone with her girls, the three of them wound tightly together, would dread any hint or whisper of a vocation—even more than I had feared to hear the ominous ring of the phone after so much loss. She had already lost her first fiancé, her mother, and then in one year, both her father and her husband. To "lose" a daughter to the cloistered life? Excruciating. Eventually, though, her loss would be the world's great gain.

---

5   Pope John Paul II, "Hope Reaching beyond the Limit," in *The Place Within: The Poetry of Pope John Paul II*, trans. Jerzy Peterkiewicz (New York: Random House, 1994), 161.

A threefold cord is not quickly broken.

— Ecclesiastes 4:12

Questions for Reflection

Have you lost anyone you've loved?

How did that affect you?

How did God resurrect your hope?

2

That Eternal Gaze

When you created these poor eyes of mine,
drawing them from the deep into your open hand,
You were thinking of that eternal gaze
enraptured by the endless deep,
and You said:
I will lower myself, brother, and never
leave your eyes in solitude.[6]

—Pope St. John Paul II

No one could ever, I think, see a photograph of our saint and not be struck immediately by the depth behind her large, dark eyes. She always loved the idea of an "abyss"—an immense depth, whether it be the chasm of her own nothingness or the profundity of God's love. And somehow, that endlessness seemed to reach from far behind her gaze. Maybe it was because, interiorly, she was constantly gazing at something, Someone, only she could see, who never left her "eyes in solitude."

Elizabeth Catez had always had striking eyes. Flashing and fiery, from the first they revealed a strong will and an unchecked temper.

[6] Pope John Paul II, "Song of the Inexhaustible Sun," in Peterkiewicz, *The Place Within*, 15.

This Present Paradise

"A real devil," her mother called her, prone to frequent tantrums and stubborn outbursts. Her parish priest observed that she would become "either a saint or a demon."[7] Perhaps we struggle with such unyielding intensity in ourselves and can thus relate to her. Maybe we have someone in our lives whose assertiveness can be both a blessing and a curse, and we can thus understand Elizabeth's mother, who was reduced at times to packing a bag with Elizabeth's things and threatening to send her to the house of corrections down the street!

None of us is completely free of this fierce tendency to grasp and control. "Every ... woman has something in herself inherited from Eve, and she must search for the way from Eve to Mary. There is a bit of defiance in each woman which does not want to humble itself under any sovereignty. In each, there is something of that desire which reaches for forbidden fruit," said St. Teresa Benedicta of the Cross (Edith Stein).[8]

But this may be even more of a struggle for someone with a choleric temperament (which Elizabeth must have had). A choleric's best assets are her iron will, determination, decisiveness, and confidence, all of which make cholerics the greatest of reformers, founders of orders, leaders—and saints. I suspect St. Teresa of Avila, the reformer of the Carmelite Order, had a choleric streak. But without conversion of heart and conformity to Christ, a choleric can be angry and domineering. Luckily, little Elizabeth would begin to surrender herself to grace before the negative traits took hold in her soul. Her "conversion," she said herself, began with her first confession.

That encounter with Christ in the sacrament of His mercy began to open her conscience, and, no longer closed in by her

---

[7] Jennifer Moorcroft: *He Is My Heaven: The Life of Elizabeth of the Trinity* (Washington, DC: ICS Publications, 2015), 9.

[8] Edith Stein: *Essays on Woman*, ed. Lucy Gelber and Romaeus Leuven, trans. Fredan Mary Oben (Washington, DC: ICS Publications, 2017), 119.

selfishness, she began to realize what her fierce and unrelenting temper was doing to those closest to her—and to her soul. She began to cooperate with grace, giving it greater space within. The interior abyss was beginning to grow. Maybe it was then her eyes began to soften a little. It was still a long road to sanctity—her mother had to threaten that she might not receive her First Holy Communion if she didn't improve—but it was a start.

Elizabeth wrote a letter to her mother on the occasion of the New Year in 1889, when she was nine years old. "I'm going to be a very gentle little girl," she wrote, "patient, obedient, conscientious, and not falling into tempers. And since I'm the elder I must set my sister a good example; I won't quarrel with her anymore, but I'll be such a little model that you'll be able to say you are the happiest of mothers, and since I hope to have the happiness of making my First Communion soon, I will be even more well-behaved, and I'll pray to God to make me even better."[9]

She would remain the same girl, with the same strong temperament, but she began to work so hard to control her anger that she would sometimes cry silently from the effort. Surrender is so painful. But she already loved the One to whom she was surrendering herself and her faults, and He was preparing her for Himself.

Then a miracle will be,
a transformation:
You will become me,
and I—eucharistic—You.[10]

—Pope St. John Paul II

[9] Letter 4, in Moorcroft, *He Is My Heaven*, 10.
[10] Pope John Paul II, "Song of the Irresistible Sun," 23.

Questions for Reflection

How does your individual personality
make holiness a challenge at times?

How has God softened or strengthened
you to make you more like Him?

What did He use to do so?

3

Never Stop Coming

The day had barely begun, and we were completely spent.

Morning Mass with preschoolers. The small crowd of mothers slumped back into the cry room after Holy Communion, looking at each other in weary camaraderie. What spirit had entered our children today, turning them into unusually wild creatures, shocking the pious elderly in the pews? The mom whose child had made a break for the altar hung her head and wondered if she could ever show her face in the church again.

I could sympathize with her. My three-year-old hadn't behaved too badly today, but not long ago, he had started belting out "Take Me Out to the Ball Game" in the Communion line in the cavernous church.

We were trying; we really were. But this was one of those days when we wondered if we really knew what we were doing.

Then our pastor stood. "I'd like to say something," he said. He was about to speak a prophetic word that would burn into our hearts like a brand of truth.

Looking into the congregation, he spoke. "I've never been at a church before where so many mothers come to daily Mass with their young children. This is a great blessing to a parish." Then he turned to us. *"Never stop coming,"* he told us emphatically, and then his voice took on a tone of conviction. "It is from your families that our future vocations will come."

I thought of this powerful moment when I read a story about little Elizabeth. When she was less than two years old, her mother took her to the South of France to visit her sick grandmother. While there, a children's Benediction service was held in the village church. Elizabeth's mother brought her to the prayer service, along with her favorite golden-haired doll, Jeannette. As they entered the church, a nun asked if they could borrow the doll as a prop to be dressed as baby Jesus and placed in a crib near the altar. I'm sure Elizabeth's mother, knowing her daughter's choleric personality, hesitated to hand Jeannette over, but the nun promised that the little girl wouldn't recognize her "baby" in the crib. So she stealthily slipped the doll to the nun and they took their place in the front row.

And yes, you can guess what happened.

The moment the priest began the service, Elizabeth caught sight of her beloved doll, dressed up and on the altar. It was too much. She screamed at the top of her voice, "Wicked priest! Give me back my Jeannette!"[11]

Oh, the humiliation! We can almost see the color rise in her mother's cheeks as she carried Elizabeth out, followed by the stares of the congregation. Nothing can mortify our pride like parenting.

But as exasperating as Elizabeth could be, her mother never gave up on her. And in her case, the words of our wise and patient pastor (who would be named a bishop the day before he gave my singing three-year-old his First Holy Communion) came true. There was a beautiful vocation buried within that shrieking toddler.

Her mother would fight that vocation, but at the same time, her careful attention to Elizabeth's religious education would also,

11 Moorcroft, *He Is My Heaven*, 5.

in a way, help to form it. Years later, Elizabeth would write to her mother from Carmel, thanking her for, first of all, introducing her to the great Carmelite saint and reformer Teresa of Avila, a favorite of Madame Catez, and, in so doing, no doubt unknowingly planting a Carmelite seed. Elizabeth also thanked her mother for "directing the heart of your little one toward Him." Her mother had pointed to the way to Jesus, and Elizabeth was forever grateful. She remembered how her mother had prepared her for her First Holy Communion, "the first encounter, that great day when we gave ourselves to each other completely!"[12]

It had been hard for her mother to let her go, harder than for most mothers, maybe, after suffering so much loss. But in the end, she would be like Abraham, ready to sacrifice his only son in Moriah, prepared to give what she loved most back to God.

"I am happy," Elizabeth wrote, "He has chosen the better part for me. Oh! Thank our great St. Teresa, whom you love so much, for the happiness of your Elizabeth."[13]

Questions for Reflection

How did your upbringing and family
of origin influence your faith?

If you are a parent, what challenges
do you face in raising your children
with their unique personalities?

---

[12] Letter 178, in Nash, Complete Works, vol. 2, 125.
[13] Letter 141, in ibid., 72.

4

Motive Makes the Saint

The formal preparation for Elizabeth's First Holy Communion would take four years — long by our current standards, but a sign that it was certainly taken seriously. These were years not only of catechism classes and guidance from her devout mother but of her own self-denial and mortification of her angry, stubborn tendencies.

When the day finally arrived, it would leave a mark on her soul forever, a signature written with a flourish in indelible ink: Jesus. Her mother noticed at the First Communion Mass that Elizabeth's tears flowed freely. The gift of tears after each Communion would continue for a long time afterward.

The space inside, carved out by her attempts to surrender herself over the previous four years, was finally filled. As they left the church the day of her First Communion, having fasted since the night before, Elizabeth confided contentedly to a friend, "I'm not hungry; Jesus has fed me."

In a child's single look
fixed on a gentle Host
I met the heavenly Father
looking at me with love.

This Present Paradise

My eyes
like some discovered flower
trembled before this gaze
in which the world was seen,
His glory beyond power.[14]

—Pope St. John Paul II

It's striking how God honors our very small efforts. This young girl, determined to master herself by setting aside her will and working on her faults, was consciously deciding to follow Christ's example of sacrifice. But she only had her daily life to offer: eating what was before her, giving way to her sister, promptly obeying her mother, putting herself aside in the choice of games when she was with her friends. Nothing big in the eyes of the world, just a few loaves and fish, but it was enough. God would accept it and take over.

It was a little leap in the purgative way—or maybe not so little, considering that those around her would notice a complete transformation of her personality from that point. Jesus lovingly knew she had done what she could. It was as if He said, *Let me take it from here.*

The Lord has laid out for us the exact means to holiness. We may look for signs in the stars, a parting of the clouds with streams of light illuminating a brilliant way to paradise, but more likely our path is made of breadcrumbs and fingerprints, pointing the way to heaven in smudges of peanut butter. It's the little things. It really is. Most of us just don't figure that out quite as early as Elizabeth did. Most of us spend years wiping counters and fingers, balancing checkbooks and babies, surrendering sleep and dreams

---

[14] Pope John Paul II, "Song of the Inexhaustible Sun," 8.

before we realize how holy it is — or rather how holy it could be, if we do it for Jesus.

Archbishop Fulton Sheen points out that

each task or duty is like a blank check; the value it possesses depends on whose name is signed to it, on whether it is done for the I's sake or for God's sake. Motive is what makes the saint: Sanctification does not depend on geography, nor on our work or circumstances.... We can take whatever He gives us, and we can make the supernatural best of it. The typist at the desk working on routine letters, the street cleaner with his broom, the farmer tilling the field with his horses, the doctor bending over the patient, the lawyer trying a case, the student with his books, the sick in their isolation and pain, the teacher drilling her pupils, the mother dressing the children — every such task, every such duty, can be ennobled and spiritualized if it is done in God's name.[15]

To pick up a pin for love can convert a soul.

—St. Thérèse of Lisieux, *Story of a Soul*

Questions for Reflection

What is God giving you today that, if you do it for love of Him, you could transform into something of supernatural value?

Whose name will you write on the check?

---

[15] Fulton J. Sheen, *Lift Up Your Heart: A Guide to Spiritual Peace* (Liguori, MO: Liguori/Triumph, 1997), 220.

5

He Played for Me

From the time I was a little girl, I loved to write. Nothing held as much promise as a smooth, new notebook, wide open and waiting for words.

Stories and poems, thoughts and prayers, all pressed with love and ink on thousands of papers in stacks of notebooks. I lost myself in words. And often, I found God waiting within them. Writing was for me an effortless, pure form of prayer. It still is. And when, by the grace of God, it touches other people, sweeping them up into a shared experience of faith or hope or love, writing becomes a particular kind of gift.

That is the beauty of a charism: a gift of the Holy Spirit, given to the individual but meant for the Church, a grace to be given away. When we were baptized, we were given all the gifts necessary for our personal sanctification. But we were also, without exception, given gifts intended for others, to be channels of God's power in the Church and in the world.

St. Elizabeth of the Trinity had an exquisite gift for music. For her, it was a holy experience to play the piano. It was a type of prayer. Others recognized her gift from the time she began playing as a child: she received awards and rave reviews, and many expected her to have a career in music. But even more, those attuned to the spiritual life recognized something divine happening when her fingers ran over the keys.

When we serve God and His people out of our giftedness, it feels fluid and free. Sometimes astonishingly fruitful things happen because it is the Holy Spirit acting, masterfully moving in and through us to the degree we allow Him. So when a saint with a charism plays music, her fingers flying over the keys and her heart sending a song heavenward, listeners follow her straight to paradise. Her music is a pure praise of God and puts people in His presence. The reason? The saint knows that in the exercise of this gift, as with all charisms, she has become the instrument. When Elizabeth was once complimented on her playing, she replied simply and humbly: "It was not I who played. He played for me."[16]

God desires that we all know the experience of being a channel of grace—of using a gift for His kingdom, to feel the freedom and joy it brings and to find ourselves operating in union with Him on a level above any ordinary human talent, elevating our experience to something beyond ourselves.

The gift itself may be humble and hidden: intercession, artistry, hospitality, service in the small things—arranging flowers for the sanctuary, gathering people around a warm and welcoming table, interceding in a particularly powerful way before the tabernacle. Or our gift may be used on a wider and more visible platform: evangelization, teaching, leading. But the results are the same. God is made manifest, hearts are renewed, and His people, drawn by a divine hunger, are moved to worship Him.

And we, the ones cooperating with the Spirit as we use our gifts, are no less blessed.

Marian T. Murphy writes in *Elizabeth of the Trinity: Her Life and Spirituality* that "Elizabeth entered so completely into her

---

[16] Mosley, *Elizabeth of the Trinity*, vol. 1, 29.

playing that she lost herself in it, becoming one with it. In the same way, she immersed herself in prayer, losing herself in God. For Elizabeth, music was not just an extension of prayer; it was prayer: love seeking expression. She confided to a friend, 'When I can no longer pray, I play!' and 'Oh, how I used to love speaking to Him that way!'"[17]

"Used to," because when she entered the Carmel, her old life, including her music, had to stay on the other side of the threshold. It was a sacrifice to let that precious part of her go, to add another little death to this new kind of life in Jesus Christ, austere and silent. This sacrifice, like all sacrifices, is never wasted. A different kind of fruit comes from setting something aside for a greater vocation. How many mothers have, even if just for a few years, had to let go of plans and promising opportunities to stay home with little souls? God is glorified in our willingness to lay down even His own gifts at His feet.

So your talents, your personality, your qualities are being wasted. So you're not allowed to take full advantage of them. Meditate well on these words of a spiritual writer: The incense offered to God is not wasted. Our Lord is more honored by the immolation of your talents than by their vain use.

—St. Josemaría Escrivá, *The Way*, no 684

Elizabeth had spent hours each day with music. But the hours of prayer now became a new kind of melody, lyrically poured out in

---

[17] Marian T. Murphy, O.C.D., *Elizabeth of the Trinity: Her Life and Spirituality* (Herefordshire, UK: Gracewing, 2011), 11.

her writings from the convent as she learned to live out of a new intensity of love and suffering. "We will also climb our calvary singing in the depths of our hearts and raising a hymn of thanksgiving to the Father,"[18] she wrote in her retreat, "Heaven in Faith."

And besides this, we know well that God will never take anything away without giving a new gift. This time, it was one of God's beautiful reversals. Now He began playing in Elizabeth's soul. She herself would become the song—a living praise to His glory. This would be the fulfillment of the gift, resurrected in a new and beautiful way. She would fall silent, and a new sound would rise.

A praise of glory is a soul of silence that remains like a lyre under the mysterious touch of the Holy Spirit so that He may draw from it divine harmonies, it knows that suffering is a string that produces still more beautiful sounds; so it loves to see this string on an instrument that it may more delightfully move the heart of its God.[19]

—St. Elizabeth of the Trinity

---

[18] St. Elizabeth of the Trinity, "Heaven in Faith," in *I Have Found God, Complete Works I*, trans. Sister Aletheia Kane, O.C.D. (Washington, DC: ICS Publications, 2014), 105.
[19] "Heaven in Faith," 112.

Questions for Reflection

What gifts has God given you to glorify
Him and sanctify the world?

How do you use those gifts most fruitfully?

Have you ever had to set those gifts
aside for a season? How was that a
sacrifice, and how did God use it?

6

I Want to Be a Nun

My dad teetered on the ladder, balancing both a paint can and a Baltimore Catechism. "Why did God make you?" he hollered down, quizzing me as I sat cross-legged on the grass underneath.

"To know Him, to love Him, and to serve Him in this world, and to be happy with Him forever in the next," I answered almost absentmindedly, watching him swipe green paint over the window frames.

Dad was determined to supplement my questionably "Catholic" education with some solid theology, even if he had to do it from the top of a ladder on a summer afternoon. And all these years later, I am grateful he did—drilling into me the basic answer to our fundamental questions: *Why am I here? What is my purpose?*

How much pain could we save ourselves if we could embrace and live the reason of our existence? It is not success, or money, or even a legacy. It is, in a word, love. We are created out of love, in love, and for love.

St. Thérèse of the Child Jesus revealed in her autobiography the moment when, distressed by her unfulfilled desires to perform the greatest deeds of all the saints, she elatedly discovered her own vocation: "I saw that all vocations are summed up in love and that love is all in all, embracing every time and place because it is eternal. In a transport of ecstatic joy, I cried: 'Jesus, my Love, I have at last found my vocation; it is love!'"[20]

And though Thérèse lived this out in a higher and more perfect way than we ever will, still, as she said, "all vocations are summed up in love." So the question for all of us is "How will I love? How will I live out this universal call in my life?"

The *Catechism of the Catholic Church* tells us that there are two primary ways:

"Both the sacrament of Matrimony and virginity for the sake of the Kingdom of God come from the Lord himself. It is he who gives them meaning and grants them the grace which is indispensable for living them out in conformity with his will (cf. Matt. 19:3–12). Esteem of virginity for the sake of the kingdom[21] and the Christian understanding of marriage are inseparable, and they reinforce each other." (1620)

Elizabeth Catez did not have to discern between the two. Even as a very little girl, she had her characteristically stubborn heart set on one vocation. She desired, more than anything, to live the prophetic mystery of spousal union as a bride of Christ.

Virginity for the sake of the kingdom of heaven is an unfolding of baptismal grace, a powerful sign of the supremacy of the bond with Christ and of the ardent expectation of his return, a sign which also recalls that marriage is a reality of this present age which is passing away.

—CCC 1619

---

[20] St. Thérèse of Lisieux, *The Story of a Soul: The Autobiography of the Little Flower* (Charlotte, NC: TAN Books, 2010), 163.
[21] Cf. LG 42; PC 12; OT 10.

I Want to Be a Nun

When she was only seven years old, Elizabeth and her mother and sister visited an old family friend, Canon Angles, the parish priest of Madame Catez's hometown. Slipping away from the children's games, Elizabeth climbed onto his knee and whispered a secret: "I want to be a nun!"

The priest, who had known her since she was a baby, could already sense something special in her and had little doubt that she had a true vocation. But someone else had overheard the conversation. And she was less than happy.

Newly widowed, Elizabeth's mother had already lost so much. The thought of surrendering her daughter too was paralyzing. She hoped that Elizabeth would forget about this "secret" and kept her as busy as possible with music lessons and studies. But little Elizabeth and her friend would sometimes sneak into the attic and, draped in her mother's long black dresses, pretend that they were nuns.

Before long, the playacting gave way to a real calling. Just before she turned fourteen, Elizabeth was making her thanksgiving after Communion and felt drawn by an irresistible invitation to take Jesus as her spouse. Right then and there, she made a vow of virginity. "We didn't say anything to each other," she recalled, "but we gave ourselves to each other by loving each other with such intense love that my determination to be wholly his became even stronger."[22]

The fact that this vow most likely occurred on July 16, the feast of Our Lady of Mount Carmel, would prove to be prophetic. But Elizabeth didn't know it yet.

Where she would live out her vocation would come to her ten days later. Again, she was praying after Communion when

[22] Moorcroft, *He Is My Heaven*, 19.

"the word Carmel was pronounced in my soul, and from then on I thought only of burying myself behind its grilles."[23]

It would be a long time before the word would become a reality. But it would be a necessary time, a time of learning to die to herself and of being willing to hand back to God even the dream of Carmel. Even our vocations, our pathways to God, are only the means to an end—the end is God Himself.

During the long wait, Elizabeth would learn that God was not confined to Carmel but already lived within her—and that, in the words of the *Baltimore Catechism*, to be happy with Him forever in the next world can begin right now, in this one.

Questions for Reflection

How does your personal state in life help you to live the vocation to love, to holiness, that we all share?

What are its particular challenges? Blessings?

How is God using them to draw you closer to Him?

23 *The Praise of Glory: Reminiscences of Sister Elizabeth of the Trinity*, trans. Benedictines of Stanbrook (London: Forgotten Books, 2015), 17.

7

Sacred Spaces

Our new house had a big bedroom for my younger sisters and me with plenty of space, two closets, and two sets of windows. I had never had my own room and never thought to ask for one — there was no "extra" room available in the bungalow, anyway, once Dad had claimed the second downstairs bedroom for his office.

But my mom had been thinking, and she saw possibilities in the space upstairs. She knew that with a few walls, I could have a quiet spot of my own. She also knew, more than I did, how much I would need one: she and I have the same quiet, introverted personality, and she had the wisdom to provide a place for me to unfold in the safety of my own small space.

So Grandpa showed up one day, with tools and drywall and determination. With wide eyes I watched him fashion two rooms out of one, and before long, with one swipe of a sliding door, I was alone. I spent many hours in that tiny room. I read, wrote, became myself. I learned to pray in that room: it was my humble little cell.

As an adult, I came to realize that it was a sacred space — that room, that house — in the sense that wherever God has worked, has done something marvelous, has mingled with us in our daily lives, *eternity puts its stamp on that place.*

This Present Paradise

It is always a wonder that a God unlimited by time and space binds Himself to it in each moment and corner where we encounter Him. And it is a fact that He creates places for us. Since Eden, He has carved out spaces and has hovered over our chaos to help us make rooms and homes, chapels and churches and places of pilgrimage that speak to us of something holy here and point to something holy beyond.

In her Carmelite classic *The Science of the Cross*, St. Edith Stein quotes St. Ambrose:

> There are places that God chooses in a special manner in order to be served there through the invocation of his name. Such was Mount Sinai, where he gave the law to Moses; in the same way, Mount Horeb, to which God sent Elijah in order to reveal himself to him there. . . . God himself knows why he chose these places in preference to others in which to receive praise. As far as we are concerned, it is enough to know that everything happens for our spiritual progress and that God listens to us there and everywhere we invoke him with perfect faith. And if we call on him in places that are especially dedicated to his service, we have a greater expectation of being heard since the Church has particularly marked and dedicated them for this purpose.[24]

Long before she entered the convent, young Elizabeth had a little corner of her room set apart and consecrated by prayer. Joanne Mosley describes it in *Elizabeth of the Trinity: The Unfolding of Her Message*: "Between the fireplace and her bed, Elizabeth had her prayer corner: an intimate and attractive space containing a prayer stool, covered in a tapestry which Madame Catez had made for her;

---

[24] Edith Stein, *The Science of the Cross*, trans. Joseph Koeppel, O.C.D. (Washington, DC: ICS Publications, 2002), 107.

also, souvenirs of her First Communion: the ivory crucifix which was framed by her blue rosary from Lourdes; and three statues, each with its own stand—the Sacred Heart, the Virgin Mary and St. Joseph."[25]

Even more than the place, though, was the time she had consecrated: the first fruits of her day, long before the household stirred. She would slip out of bed and kneel before Jesus, beginning the day the same way she would continue it: in dialogue with the One she loved. Like the wise virgins, she kept her lamp lit in the hours before dawn. "How many matches I was obliged to hide, to avoid inconvenient questions!"[26] she admitted years later.

Who can guess what conversations went on in that tiny retreat? We know that Elizabeth was already longing for a cell in the convent she could see from the window in that very room, and I'm sure she spent many mornings asking for the gift to make that her home.

But Jesus would give this girl a different grace first, one she needed to know before she could take her place in the convent. This grace is one we all need, and unknown to Elizabeth at the time, it would become the message of her life.

She became aware that there was a cell in her soul, designed by the Holy Spirit, one where she could hold constant vigil, with a little sanctuary lamp burning continually in her heart. Jesus had made His home there—and with or without Carmel, she could hide away with Him even in the midst of the world she longed to leave. "Make yourself a cell in your soul and never leave it," St. Catherine of Siena said. St. Catherine never lived in a convent: she was a laywoman very much wrapped up in the world, caring for the destitute and involved in politics and in negotiating family feuds and even religious dissension within the highest ranks

[25] Mosley, *Elizabeth of the Trinity*, vol. 1, 30.
[26] Ibid., 47.

of the Church. But she fiercely protected the sacred silent space inside of her.

I believe this was one reason Jesus asked Elizabeth to wait. It was to teach her a truth so that she could teach us. He wanted her to experience the reality of His life within her, of their communion in the secret recesses of her soul, unshakably true and unchanging, no matter where she was or what her state of life. He wanted her to taste the truth of eternal space in her soul while she was busy with the stuff of daily life so that she could know how to spoon it out to the rest of us.

Yes, finally, she would enter the Carmel down the street—steps away and yet a world apart. Hans Urs von Balthasar writes, "When Elizabeth first becomes acquainted with her cell, she has an immediate impression of falling barriers and disappearing bars."[27] "My Three are present here!"[28] she cried as the door swung open. All of heaven in a stark room, Christ without confines. "My horizon," she said, "grows larger each day."[29] Finally, her surroundings reflected her interior life, where everything was ordered toward encountering His limitless love.

Still, she had to tell those left in the world what they could have too. To her young friend Françoise, she wrote, "You must build a little cell within your soul as I do. Remember that God is there and enter it from time to time; when you feel nervous or you're unhappy, quickly seek refuge there and tell the Master all about it."[30]

The reality is that it is in our little spaces, some outside, some inside, where eternity opens up to us. Little portals into immensity itself. And we can no longer cling to what is shallow or "clutch at

[27] Hans Urs von Balthasar, *Two Sisters in the Spirit* (San Francisco: Ignatius Press, 1992), 425.
[28] Mosley, *Elizabeth of the Trinity*, vol. 1, 166.
[29] Letter 89, in Nash, *Complete Works*, vol. 2, 17.
[30] Letter 123, in ibid., 123.

straws"—to use a phrase of St. Thérèse—for we have peered into places we cannot describe.

Questions for Reflection

Do you have a time and place consecrated for prayer?

How has God used that time and place to
deepen your relationship with Him?

If not, where could you create such a place?

How might that change your prayer life?

8

Between Two Worlds

The sound of the bells of the Carmelite convent, just around the corner from Elizabeth's house, must have seemed a constant reminder of the vow of virginity she had made as a child and the whisper of "Carmel" with which the Lord replied. Elizabeth's desire for this life with Jesus grew greater each day. Finally, around the time she turned sixteen, Elizabeth got up the courage to approach her mother about entering the convent.

We can image her vulnerability at that moment. All her precious dreams, cherished secretly, now held out in trembling hope to someone who could receive them gently or crush them abruptly. Decisively, the answer came: *no.* She must not think of it, at least not for years. And not only that: she was no longer allowed to attend Mass at the convent or visit with the nuns there. Her heart twisted in pain at this awful answer—to be cut off completely from not only the dream but every contact with the cloister.

And so began her exile. "Why do you make me languish?"[31] she moaned in a private poem to Jesus. She put up a good front because she had mastered herself enough not to reveal the storm inside, but her pain was raw. She wrestled between two worlds, called to one

---

[31] Poem 29, in *Elizabeth of the Trinity*, vol. 1, 45.

but confined to the other. Peace was as far away as the promised land, and this sea showed no sign of parting.

Many of us can relate to the experience of having doors close us off from what we genuinely believe to be God's will. We are ready to rush into careers, parenthood, marriages, moves, missions—our hearts bursting with the desire to serve Him in great ways, and God whispers, "Wait." It's tempting to stamp our foot and demand, "Don't You need me? I gave You my life!" After a time, we realize that, yes, He has accepted our lives, *but He also wants our wills*. That means giving back to Him what matters most. And this is a greater, interior crucifixion.

St. Gianna Molla, who surrendered missionary dreams for motherhood, had this to say: "What is a vocation? It is a gift from God and therefore comes from God. If then it is a gift from God, it is up to us to do all in our power to know God's will. We must go along that way, if God wills it, not forcing the door; when God wills it, how God wills it."[32]

A friend of mine confided in me of her struggle in living between vocations. She had discerned after some time in the convent that religious life was not her calling, but marriage had not materialized yet. As one decade unfolded into another, she ached for fulfillment but found only a long stretch of seemingly inexplicable delay. I looked at her hands, clutched in her lap, and said the one thing that came to mind: *Waiting is a kind of suffering*. I think this empty time is an early spring when life is pressing on the soil from below but cannot yet break out. It is a time to be available but not employed. It is to be the day laborer who has not been called into the field. It is necessary, and it is hard.

And so this waiting, this suffering, this time of testing would become arguably the most important in Elizabeth's life, a precious

[32] "Vocational Search," Saint Gianna Beretta Molla, https://saint-gianna.org/vocsearsh.htm.

period when God's wisdom began to be manifest and she began to understand the beauty and the greater good of *God's will*. She had the virtue of obedience and knew that God's will was wrapped in her mother's response. So she learned to die to her desires and come to a place of purifying surrender. She realized that the only thing in her power was loving His will in each moment as it came to her—and for now, that will was very clearly not in Carmel.

Later, her mother became very sick, and Elizabeth had to resign herself to the possibility that she would never enter. It fell to her, as the oldest daughter, to care for her widowed mother as long as she was needed. This was the greatest test. In the end, she was not asked to carry that cross. Still, she held out her hands for it, she turned around and bent over, ready to shoulder the heaviest burden she knew. She was still under the weight of God's will—like St. Frances of Rome, who put her wishes for religious life aside when challenged by her confessor: "Are you crying because you want to do God's will or because you want God to do your will?"

It was Jesus who was working in Elizabeth's heart, challenging her: "Are you able to drink the cup that I am to drink?" (Matt. 20:22). It was Jesus, who had taught her to pray and who teaches all of us to say: *Our Father, Who art in Heaven, hallowed be Thy name; Thy Kingdom come. Thy will be done on earth as it is in Heaven.* It was Jesus, who modeled for us what it meant to be fully surrendered to Love: "Father, if it be possible, let this cup pass from me; nevertheless, not as I will, but as thou wilt" (Matt. 26:39).

To say and mean "Thy Will be done" is to put an end to all complaining; for whatever the moment brings to us now bears the imprint of the Divine Will.

—Archbishop Fulton Sheen, *Lift Up Your Heart*

This Present Paradise

Elizabeth wrote another poem, and this time there were no questions: "May your will be done/ And may it be blessed forever."[33] *The delay was not an obstacle to God's plan. It was part of it.* It would be the place of a deep encounter with Christ's Cross and an occasion of learning both to trust God and to offer herself for others. It was a gift, and she was beginning to unwrap it.

Years later, while filling out the postulant's questionnaire, she was asked, "What name would you like to have in heaven?" Her answer said it all: *Will of God.*

Take, Lord, and receive all my liberty,
my memory, my understanding,
and my entire will,
all I have and call my own.
You have given all to me.
To You, Lord, I return it.
Everything is Yours; do with it what You will.
Give me only Your love and Your grace,
That is enough for me.

—St. Ignatius of Loyola, Suscipe

---

33 Poem 44, in Mosley, *Elizabeth of the Trinity*, vol. 1, 55.

Questions for Reflection

How does God reveal His will to you?

What circumstances or dreams might God be asking you to surrender to His will?

How does He give you the grace to do so?

Can you think of other saints who had to give up a dream for something greater?

9

And God Saw That It Was Good

If the doorbell was rung with wild abandon on a weekend morning, we all knew who was there. Flying downstairs, we'd find our beloved bachelor uncle, grinning through his beard with an invitation to join him on an excursion into nature. Any given Sunday could find us watching Canada geese gather at the marsh, following a hiking trail in a state forest, biking along Lake Michigan, fishing, or skating on a frozen pond.

I treasure the memories of those childhood adventures: crunching through the leaves at the trailhead, hiking the golden hills of the moraine, watching the sun set over the lake, gazing at hundreds of wild geese swimming through the cattails.

Words alone cannot make a writer. Beauty makes a writer: impressing lovely things like warm wax on a child's heart; and from the overflowing wonder, words can't help but pour out.

My first childish attempts at writing tried to capture a little bit of nature's radiance:

> Just as the sun was about to be swallowed by
>   the evening sky,
> it spilled across the horizon
> and splashed across our surprised faces,

our last lick, dripping us in
blood-red mercy before
it drained
down the throat of the star-freckled night.

Sometimes our outings would end with a stop to visit the pinnacle of creation: we would find a chapel and kneel before Jesus hidden in the Host.

This was the Word Himself, who, spoken over the world, had unfurled the light, poured forth the waters, rolled out the hills, separated seasons, swiped them with color, and painted the forests. This was the center of everything, I knew even as a little girl. The glories of nature exist to reveal and glorify Him, and we can see His imprint everywhere.

Elizabeth knew this too. The early summers of her life included long stretches of travel, allowing her to gaze at gorgeous views that mirrored the expanse opening in her heart. Her earliest poems reflect inner and outer vistas:

How great, how beautiful,
This nature is, O my God!
So how good it is, in the midst of nature,
To raise one's soul to heaven![34]

When on the welcoming shores
Dashing at my feet
The blue waves come
It is nice to dream and pray![35]

---

[34] Poem 9, in ibid., 35.

[35] Poem 14, in *Elizabeth of the Trinity* by Sister Giovanna Della Croce, O.C.D., trans. Julie Enzler (Manchester, NH: Sophia Institute Press, 2016), 15.

And God Saw That It Was Good

In the mountains, she wrote that she "was in ecstasy" over the rushing "diamonds" of a waterfall; she relished the beauty of the peaks, the trees, the moonlight. Her first look at the Atlantic Ocean thrilled her. "It's wonderful, and I can't tell you what a superb sight it is," she wrote. "I love that boundless, limitless horizon! Mother and Guite couldn't drag me away from my contemplation of it."[36] "I love the countryside," she said.[37]

It was in part her growing faith that made even the stuff of the earth seem lovelier. Prayer makes us more alive. It makes life richer, color more vivid, sounds clearer, light brighter, joy deeper, sorrow sweeter. It is not compartmentalized into a spiritual square, stacked away in a closet to be pulled out in a quiet time, but is messy, in a beautiful way, spilling out over life like sunshine. And Elizabeth was wholly alive, embracing the world with true joy.

But if her mother hoped that the taste of all the freshness and beauty of the world could entice her to remain in it, she would be disappointed. Even her stanzas end with contemplating higher things. Elizabeth loved the created world, but she loved its Creator and Redeemer more. Her inner world was beautiful too, and she wanted to live alone with Jesus in that hidden, radiant place.

Still, in those years of waiting before the convent doors opened to her, it must have been refreshment for her soul to be able to absorb all of God's goodness in the open expanses of the country. Though she was locked in and limited by her mother's resistance, something of God's peace and providential care must have washed over her when she looked out over all that He had made.

He ordered all things in His care to Himself, and she knew that included her. The God who set light apart from dark and water apart from land had set her apart for Himself. He was not sleeping; He

---

[36] Letter 30, in Moorcroft, *He Is My Heaven*, 54.
[37] Letter 30, in Mosley, *Elizabeth of the Trinity*, vol. 1, 123.

was moving over her life, just as He had hovered over the waters during Creation. And He would gather her up into the sea of His love exactly when she was ready.

When she entered Carmel, her window to the world would constrict, but she still admired its beauty in slivers: "The sky is beautiful, all clear and starry," she wrote one winter; "the moonlight is flooding our cell through the frosted window panes, it's ravishing."[38]

She remembered nature in a letter to her sister who was on a vacation in Switzerland: "It seems a long time since we climbed the mountains together; I remember what a lovely view we had from our room. Don't you find that nature speaks to you of God?"[39]

And late in her life, when she became sick, she was sent outside to sit in the fresh air to try to regain her health. From the balcony, she contemplated creation. "All nature seems so full of God to me: the wind blowing in the tall trees, the little birds singing, the beautiful blue sky, everything speaks to me of Him."[40]

My home is no longer the landscape of Wisconsin, with its alternating seasons of white and green and the riot of colored leaves. God has drawn me into the desert of the Southwest now, with a starker kind of beauty: a single lush, fragile bloom on the tip of a thorny cactus, a red mountain dusted with brush, the drifting scent of orange blossoms in the spring. No one rings my doorbell anymore to call me out of myself, but now and then Jesus lifts me out of my worries and sticky to-do lists to marvel at His magnificence. Looking up, I can't help but feel secure in His hugeness. God is God, and He is doing mighty things, in the world and in my life — and in your life. Your soul is more valuable than all the mountains and

---

[38] Letter 187, in Nash, *Complete Works*, vol. 2, 138.
[39] Letter 210, in ibid., 170.
[40] Letter 236, in ibid., 210.

forests and seas and all the life teeming within them—infinitely so, because it bears His image.
And God saw that it was *very good.*

The wilderness and the dry land shall be glad,
the desert shall rejoice and blossom;
like the crocus, it shall blossom abundantly,
and rejoice with joy and singing.
The glory of Lebanon shall be given to it,
the majesty of Carmel and Sharon.
They shall see the glory of the LORD,
the majesty of our God.

— Isaiah 35:1–2

Questions for Reflection

How does beauty reveal God to you or
help you experience His glory?

What places of beauty have drawn your heart to God?

Do you see your soul as God's masterpiece?

10

Expect Him Everywhere

Even as a little girl, Elizabeth had a Eucharistic heart.

A transformation had taken place after her First Communion and a deeper life had begun to grow, spilling out in her eyes, in her prayer, in her life. It really was a union of Jesus with His Elizabeth. They were growing closer and closer, and she was recognizing His voice in her depths. It was immediately after receiving the Eucharist, while He was still physically present within her, that she heard first the call to become His as a consecrated religious and then to enter Carmel.

Already she was on the way to incarnating the words of St. Edith Stein (Teresa Benedicta of the Cross):

In order to have Divine Love as its inner form, a woman's life must be a Eucharistic life. Only in daily, confidential relationship with the Lord in the tabernacle can one forget self, become free of all wishes and pretensions, and have a heart open to the needs and wants of others. Whoever lets herself be purified by the sanctifying power coming from the sacrifice of the altar, offering herself to the Lord in this sacrifice, whoever receives the Lord in her soul's innermost depth in Holy Communion cannot but be drawn ever more deeply and powerfully into the divine life, incorporated into the Mystical Body of Christ, her heart converted to the likeness of the divine heart."[41]

A woman's life must be a Eucharistic life.

What does that mean, to "have Divine Love as its inner form"? Well, as a philosopher, St. Teresa Benedicta was referring to the "inner form" as the force behind all the other virtues, which binds them, animates them, coordinates them, and makes them fruitful. It is the director of our souls. What do we want directing our soul if not Divine Love? And so our lives must be Eucharistic. "Everything, in the plan of Redemption, is based on the *Eucharistic life* as much as it is upon the rock of Peter,"[42] says Jean-Baptiste Chautard in his classic work, *The Soul of the Apostolate*.

Elizabeth wrote, "It seems to me that nothing better expresses the love in God's Heart than the Eucharist; it is union, consummation, He in us, we in Him, and isn't that Heaven on Earth?"[43] She received Jesus in the Blessed Sacrament as often as possible. According to the common practice at the time, she could not receive every day. But she longed for Him, hungered for Him, desired Him. She was overjoyed when her priest allowed her to receive four times a week, rather than three. And when her confessor allowed her Communion every day for the eight days of the Corpus Christi Octave in June of 1898, she savored the continuous encounter. Two years later, she was again able to receive for eight days in observance of the feast of Teresa of Avila. As it ended, she wrote, "O my God, you are sending me the greatest of sacrifices! Having received you every day, what is going to become of me without

---

[41] Stein, *Essays on Woman*, 56.
[42] Jean-Baptiste Chautard, O.C.S.O., *The Soul of the Apostolate* (Charlotte, NC: TAN Books, 2012), 24.
[43] Letter 165, in Nash, *Complete Works*, vol. 2, 105.

you? But, you have told me, you have no need of the Sacrament to come to me!"[44]

You have no need of the Sacrament to come to me.

I'll never forget when this hit me with a force I'll never forget.

One Sunday, I had hoped to get away to spend some time — not even an hour, just a little time — in the adoration chapel in a nearby parish. But it wasn't meant to be. Little fires had to be put out, the many needs of six children simply had to be attended to, and soon the day was gone. Finally, that night, I knelt. Not in prayer. I knelt on the kitchen floor, head bent, cleaning up spilled Cheerios. And then, suddenly, this:

You couldn't come to me, so I have come to you.

The words penetrated my heart. He was there. He was there, with me, among my mess in the dark kitchen. He saw. He knew.

Imagine the surge in my heart when, years later, I came across these words in a letter Elizabeth wrote to her sister, Guite, who couldn't make it to Mass on Holy Thursday, the day after her second baby was born: "I've carried your soul with mine everywhere during this great week, especially during the night of Holy Thursday, and since you could not go to Him, I told Him to come to you."[45]

Jesus knows our hearts and our efforts. He chooses ordinarily to come to us through the powerful means He has given, but He is not confined by them. When the obligations and restrictions of our vocation and our God-given circumstances conflict with our desires, even our holy desires, it is simply another opportunity to be a little white flag in His wind. And that, really, is all He needs to see to sweep in and become our greatest desire.

He will come as He will. Make plans to meet Him whenever you can — but *expect Him everywhere.*

---

[44] Mosley, *Elizabeth of the Trinity*, vol. 1, 129.
[45] Letter 227, in Nash, *Complete Works*, vol. 2, 198.

This Present Paradise

The Church gives us a powerful practice whenever we cannot receive Communion physically: an Act of Spiritual Communion. This is the kind of communion Elizabeth practiced until it became as natural as breathing: *Jesus in, self out. Jesus in, self out, Jesus in, self out.* "We will breathe in love and draw it down on souls and on the whole Church."[46]

Act of Spiritual Communion
My Jesus,
I believe that You
are present in the Most Holy Sacrament.
I love You above all things,
and I desire to receive You into my soul.
Since I cannot at this moment
receive You sacramentally,
come at least spiritually into my heart.
I embrace You as if You were already there
and unite myself wholly to You.
Never permit me to be separated from You.
Amen.

Questions for Reflection
Have you ever been deprived of the sacraments?

How did God send you His presence
and His grace in that season?

Does the Eucharist occupy a deep
place in your devotion?

---

[46] Letter 214, in ibid., 180.

11

The Woman of the Hour

"You belong to me."

Chills went down my spine as I listened to a talk on spiritual warfare. The priest explained how the Eastern Church Fathers taught that, at the hour of our death, we can expect the greatest temptations of our lives. A temptation tailor-made for us, based on our sins and weaknesses. The priest reminded us that on her deathbed, even St. Thérèse had a momentary temptation to suicide because her physical suffering from tuberculosis was so great.

Satan's last-ditch effort, he said, will be to remind us of our sins and say, "You belong to me."

Almost immediately, though, as the priest went on talking, I imagined another voice in those final moments—a woman's voice. A voice that with unmistakable authority would say: "No. She belongs to me" and would definitively send all evil away with a word.

Pray for us sinners now and at the hour of our death. We ask this every time we say the Hail Mary.

But I was specifically thinking about my Marian Consecration. I was thinking of how, many times over the years, I had consecrated myself to Jesus through Our Lady, in effect saying yes to her assistance in helping me live out my baptismal promises to the very end, to fulfill my Christian vocation.

This Present Paradise

Jesus gave Our Lady to us at the Cross, but she, who said "fiat" in complete freedom at the Annunciation and at the Cross (and many times in between) also waits for our yes and respects our free will. She stands with arms outstretched, waiting for us to run to her as our Mother. Our consecration of ourselves to her is our falling into her embrace and saying: *Yes, Mama. I am your child. Help me.*

The year 2017 was the hundredth anniversary of the Fatima apparitions, and to honor Our Lady that year, I took a large parish group through the *33 Days to Morning Glory* consecration developed by Fr. Michael Gaitley.[47] Our pastor came to speak one night during our preparation and reminded us of something striking. "You can consecrate anything to Mary that rightly belongs to you," he said. "Your home, your business, your children, your marriage. I can consecrate this parish because of my authority as pastor. But I can't consecrate the diocese — the bishop would have to do that. The pope can consecrate the world." (In fact, the bishop would consecrate our diocese that year in a packed cathedral. Two years later, our pastor would consecrate our parish.)

This really got me thinking. What belonged to me that I could give to Mary?

One day, while searching for something in a drawer, I came across an old prayer journal. When I picked it up, two slips of paper fell out and landed at my feet. I unfolded them and saw their significance: they were signed copies of the Marian Consecration my husband and I had made ten years before. I looked closer and realized in amazement that, in exactly one week, it would be the ten-year anniversary of that consecration. I knew that my husband and I needed to renew our consecration on the anniversary of that

---

[47] Michael E. Gaitley, M.I.C., *33 Days to Morning Glory* (Stockbridge, MA: Marian Press, 2011).

date. And so, a week later we prayed, heads bent together, to surrender to Mary not only ourselves and our marriage but our family
as well—the most precious thing we had we gave her.

St. Elizabeth of the Trinity also had something that she treasured deeply.

She had her vocation.

She had already surrendered even that to the will of God. For
safekeeping, during very doubtful years, she tucked it into Mary's
hands. What else could she do?

She wrote a poem to Our Lady of Lourdes, confident in the
power of her intercession:

> It is you who will have obtained for me …
> The joy, at last of being His bride,
> This title of which I am so jealous;
> But may His will be mine!
> Oh! that is what you must obtain for me![48]

Elizabeth believed it would be Mary who would obtain the
permission of her earthly mother and give her the freedom to
enter the convent. But, as we've seen before, in her deepening
humility she begged that Mary would obtain for her, even more
than Carmel, the great grace of being utterly united with the will
of God. After all, it was Our Lady alone who never wavered from
God's will.

And so, in that sense, she gave something greater than her
vocation to her Heavenly Mother: she handed over her will.

On February 2, 1899, the feast of the Presentation of the Lord,
Elizabeth once again presented herself and her vocation to Mary.
"On every Marian feast, I renew my consecration to the heavenly
Mother.... Today I entrusted my future and my vocation to her.

---

[48] Poem 53, in *Complete Works*, vol. 1, 63.

Yes, because Jesus doesn't want me yet, His will be done, but I will grow holy in the world."⁴⁹

Jesus doesn't want me yet. When would her hour come?

Elizabeth must have remembered that in the Gospel it is Mary who effectively decides the hour when Jesus would begin His public ministry with the miracle in Cana (John 2:1–11).

During the preparation for our parish consecration, we were discussing Cana, and a woman's hand shot up. She confessed that Christ's words "O woman, what have you to do with me? My hour has not yet come" sounded harsh to her, and she really struggled to understand His meaning.

But, of course, Jesus was not being harsh with His Mother. He was asking a question regarding the reality of His public ministry. What He was saying was: *Are we really going to do this now? This isn't supposed to be the time yet. Are you ready for this? Because you and I both know what this means. This will be the beginning of the end. And it will involve both of us. It has everything to do with you, the "Woman," and me.*

Mary, who brought Him into the world, would accompany Him even unto His death, participating in His sacrifice in a way far beyond any other human being and therefore participating in our salvation so profoundly that she would be called *Co-Redemptrix.*

When she says to the servants, "Do whatever He tells you," she says that it *is* time. The woman who brought Him back from the Temple when He was twelve, who said then, in effect, "No, it's not time yet," now throws open the door to the rest of the story and walks through it with Him. And from that point on, every step they took together would be one step closer to the Cross. And they both knew it.

---

⁴⁹ Della Croce, *Elizabeth of the Trinity*, 20.

The Woman of the Hour

And so Elizabeth, in entrusting her vocation to the "Woman of the Hour," allowed Mary to decide if and when she would enter Carmel. She waited for Mary to speak into her mother's heart, "She has no wine" when Elizabeth was thirsting for the solitude of the convent. She knew that Our Lady would orchestrate everything perfectly as long as Elizabeth would be patient and "do whatever He tells you." And, of course, she did. They both did.

Not two months after Elizabeth had handed over her vocation, the Blessed Mother handed it back to her.

In an astonishing concession, after Elizabeth's sympathetic sister, Guite, had once again raised the subject with their mother about her older sister's vocation, Madame Catez announced that Elizabeth would be allowed to enter Carmel after all. She would need to wait another two years, until she was twenty-one, but the permission was granted.

"Truly, it must be Mary who has gained this grace for me,"[50] Elizabeth wrote in her journal later that day, probably still spinning at the sudden reversal. "O Mary, thank you, I am so moved, I can only say one word—*merci*."[51]

Questions for Reflection

Have you consecrated yourself to the Blessed Mother?

What else could you entrust to her?

How has Our Lady brought you closer to her Son?

[50] Moorcroft, *He Is My Heaven*, 38.
[51] Mosley, *Elizabeth of the Trinity*, vol. 1, 89.

12

Headaches and Hair Shirts

One of my theology professors in college encouraged my class to add fasting to our prayer. But he had a caveat that came from his own experience. "I used to fast all day on Fridays," he said. "And when I'd come home from work, I'd be so weak and tired I'd have to lie down." This was a problem because he was a father with young children at home.

His wife, who had lived, perhaps, a much greater mortification that day homeschooling their large family, would have appreciated some relief and help at dinnertime. Instead, he was resting, drained from his voluntary penance while she juggled dinner, toddlers, and her own tiredness.

His intentions? Noble and generous. But completely disordered. Eventually, his wife was forced to confront him.

His first priority should have been his vocation, his state in life. He had obligations to fill at home and by neglecting them, even for good reasons, he was hurting those who had the first claim to his time and energy. "Don't do what I did," he told us ruefully, shaking his head.

This Present Paradise

Choose mortifications that don't mortify others.

— St. Josemaría Escrivá, *The Way*, no. 179

Mortifications are those acts of self-denial that subdue our bodily desires for comfort. The word "mortification" comes from the Latin *mortificationem*, which means "a killing, or a putting to death." The goal is to be detached enough even from our own bodies to give of ourselves in a complete way in imitation of Christ crucified.

But the primary way we are to give of ourselves is within our vocation. A mother's giving her body over for her growing child within; a father's long hours of work to provide for the little souls at home; a priest's rising in the night to anoint a dying person — these come before anything else. The duties of our vocation are a way to sanctity that we don't need to guess at. We just need to embrace them. They are a practical kind of penance. And sometimes the obedience to our state in life requires the mortification of our will more than anything else.

There have been times I would have liked to pray longer. But the child climbing into my lap, wanting to know what's for breakfast — that's my mortification (and a wonderful one)! I would gladly have gone on a pilgrimage, tracing the steps of saints and sacrificing the comfort of home to pray in holy places. But maybe I'm just supposed to follow the crumbs to the kitchen and help the first grader sound out his spelling words. That's my will, given over for the other.

Anything that compromises my calling is a false kind of penance and outside of God's will. The greater suffering sometimes is *not being able to choose our own suffering*.

St. Elizabeth of the Trinity, before she entered the convent, would have loved to embrace a strict life of penance in addition to her rich prayer life. In her fervent love, there was little she wouldn't have sacrificed for Jesus. She wanted to unite herself to Him in His Passion. It was certainly one of the things that drew her to the Carmelites because the simple but severe life of a Carmelite is one of intense mortification of the flesh. The way of Carmel is really the road to Calvary.

"My Savior," she wrote, "I desire to return Thee love for love, blood for blood. Thou didst die for me, therefore I will endure fresh sufferings for Thee, every day shall bring me some fresh martyrdom because of my deep love for Thee."[52]

But there was a problem. It was becoming evident that Elizabeth was increasingly unwell, which could have prevented her from entering the convent. She spoke to the prioress in Dijon, Mother Marie, who pressed her about her practices. And then it became clear: in Elizabeth's desire to suffer for Christ, this otherwise healthy twenty-year-old was putting her own calling at risk. She had prayed for the impression of the crown of thorns and was secretly wearing a hair shirt, which was keeping her awake at night! She was tortured by headaches and unable to sleep, and her health was deteriorating. Immediately Mother Marie told her "to pray that her trial might be ended"[53] and ordered her to stop wearing the hair shirt. She obeyed, and once she was able to get adequate sleep, her health returned.

What had seemed like a good idea was actually stealing away her health and inhibiting her freedom to fulfill her vocation, even as the long-awaited date grew closer. This was not God's will, and through the wisdom of the prioress, she was able to get back on course. What a disaster it would have been if she hadn't been able to join the Carmelites, all because of a hair shirt!

---

[52] *The Praise of Glory*, 47.
[53] Ibid.

This Present Paradise

She learned her lesson well enough to pass it on years later in her letters. "Forgetting yourself with respect to your health does not mean neglecting to take care of yourself, for that is your duty and your best of penances," she noted to her friend.[54] To her sister, a tired mom with two little girls, she wrote, "I beg you to be very wise and sleep well, you need that so much."[55]

Sometimes sacrifices are good and right and fit within our existing commitments. Sometimes they stretch us but still allow us to take care of what we've already been entrusted with. Sometimes a challenging new call develops as seasons and obligations change. But what if we take on what seems like a good thing, and other important things begin to crumble? Then it's time to reevaluate. Sometimes the enemy of our souls offers us something good because he wants to steal something great: "even Satan disguises himself as an angel of light" (2 Cor. 11:14).

Thankfully Elizabeth had a guide with the wisdom to mortify her with obedience rather than severe physical penances. God would provide physical suffering later.

But for now, He just wanted her ready to enter Carmel. And that meant a good night's sleep.

Come away ... and rest a while.

—Mark 6:31

---

[54] Letter 249, in Nash, *Complete Works*, vol. 2, 229.
[55] Letter 239, in Nash, *Complete Works*, vol. 2, 215.

Questions for Reflection

Have you ever taken on a penance that interfered with other obligations? What happened?

What sacrifices, fitting within your state of life, might the Lord be asking of you now?

13

Shiny Things

This Advent, I vowed, would be different. I would live it as a season of preparation, my heart watchful and as still as an empty manger. I would be prayerful and patient, keeping my lamps lit and my ways straight. I would bypass commercialism and materialism and keep my head bowed and my eyes fixed on the coming Christ Child. I was ready.

And then I went to the mall.

There I found the crush of the crowds, the signs screaming sales, the blaring music, the confusion in my mind as I sifted through piles of sweaters and socks, swiped credit cards, and tried to keep my eyes off those distractingly adorable shoes that would look so good with that dress.

Soon I was as crumpled as the tattered list in my hand, both interiorly and exteriorly. I was unraveled and disheveled and curiously empty even though my bags were full. I slumped home, defeated for the moment—but determined to recapture some peace.

I scooped up the kids who ran to me for a quick hug, stashed the bags, and started dinner. As the chicken simmered, I thought about one of the books my daughter had recently been assigned in school: *Black Beauty*. While we had read together, snuggled on the couch, one scene had struck me particularly.

This Present Paradise

Black Beauty, in reminiscing about his training, recalled one thing that was "a very great advantage." His wise and experienced master intentionally brought him to a neighbor's farm, which was bordered on one side by a railway.

The young horse innocently began to graze with the other animals when, all of a sudden, a train flew by—the first one he had seen—noisy, clattering, filling the air with unfamiliar smoke. He ran to the other side of the field, stunned and frightened. As the days went by, he could find no peace in the constant threat of such commotion but then noticed that the cows, used to the shrieking and groaning of the engines, barely raised their heads as the trains rushed by. And soon he found that he, too, could ignore them. For the rest of his life, he said he could be "as fearless at railway stations as in my own stable."

"Now if anyone wants to break in a young horse well," he reflected, "that is the way."[56]

Maybe that is how we should look at the distractions, advertisements, and chaos of the world. Maybe these are opportunities to practice self-mastery and recollection—to keep our center in Christ even as the surrounding noise beckons us away from Him and closer to the edge of self-indulgence.

It is easy (well, easier) to remain focused when in a candlelit Church or tucked away in a prayer corner. But taking Christ with us when we enter the store or the office or the party? That is the challenge. And it is one that can be overcome only with practice —and grace.

But if we're not called to the cloister, then we're called to practice recollection in the middle of a noisy and scattered life and to pray that we perfect it. Practicing recollection is one of the keys to holiness in a world that would love to claim us for itself and that

---

[56] Anna Sewell, *Black Beauty* (New York: Penguin, 2011), 12–13.

leaves shiny things everywhere to lead us away from the path to God. The world sings a siren song through the Internet or the radio or the podcast or the empty conversations. That is a not-so-subtle tactic of the enemy of our souls. "Noise," says the demon in the *Screwtape Letters*, "the grand dynamism, the audible expression of all that is exultant, ruthless, and virile.... We will make the whole universe a noise in the end. We have already made great strides in this direction as regards the Earth."[57]

It is a world that roars past us with the force of a steam engine, that pulls and drags us away from the Prince of Peace because it does not know Him. But we do. And we want to stay with Him always.

We also have a wise and experienced Master who will allow us to be in very distracting and even scary places where He seems far way — precisely so we will have the opportunity to discover and remember Him in the center of our souls, to resist the lesser magnetic forces drawing us into distraction, and to find a deeper weight in our own being anchoring us to something lasting. Eventually we won't even look up when the world comes calling with its wares. "And when no outer rest is attainable," sympathizes St. Edith Stein, "when there is no place in which to retreat, if pressing duties prohibit a quiet hour, then at least she must for a moment seal herself inwardly against all other things and take refuge in the Lord. He is indeed there and can give us in a single moment what we need."[58] We'll realize that what is outside of us can have no hold on us when we are firmly present to God within. Spiritual blinders keep our internal eyes on the one thing necessary.

[57] C.S. Lewis, *The Screwtape Letters*, annotated ed. (New York: HarperOne, 2013), 132.
[58] Stein, *Essays on Woman*, 144.

This Present Paradise

Why do you look around you, if you
carry "your world" within you?

—St. Josemaría Escrivá, *The Way*, no. 184

St. Elizabeth of the Trinity carried her world within her. Before she entered the convent, she was obligated to attend dances and parties. She went willingly, knowing how much it meant to her mother. She mortified her own desire for silence out of charity and obedience to Madame Catez, who was hoping that a taste of the world might persuade her daughter to stay in it. Elizabeth was totally at ease in society and a joy to be around, but she kept an inner silence and took God within her even into the swirl of society. Her friend related: "She was not worldly and yet she presented herself in a room with an ease, a distinction, a grace, an amiableness which charmed everyone. Her expression was animated, her beautiful gaze illuminated, her conversation was always full of liveliness and always so charitable to everyone. From the first moment, she cut an imposing figure through something interior, personal, and through her marvelous self-possession."[59]

Remaining with Jesus deep within wasn't always easy. She admitted in her diary, "I often leave Thee as lonely as if Thou were in the desert!" But she prayed for the grace to be wholly His, without any piece of her heart scattering itself in any worldly distractions: "May my life be a continual prayer, a long act of love. May nothing distract me from You, no noise or distractions. I would so love, my Master, to live with You in silence. But what I love above all is to do Your will, and since You want me to be in the world at present, I submit myself with all my heart for love of You. I offer You the

---

[59] Mosley, *Elizabeth of the Trinity*, vol. 1, 112–113.

cell of my heart to be your little Bethany; come and live there, I love You so much."[60]

It was obvious to others that there was something different in our saint. A woman noticed an otherworldly look in her eyes, even as dancers whirled around her at a party.

"Elizabeth," she said, "you see God."[61]

Questions for Reflection

What things are most distracting to you?

What disturbs your peace or invades your prayer?

What can you do to begin to reclaim
your inner recollection?

---

[60] Moorcroft, *He Is My Heaven*, 47.
[61] Mosley, *Elizabeth of the Trinity*, vol. 1, 114.

14

Works of Mercy

"In those days Mary arose and went with haste into the hill country, to a city of Judah, and she entered the house of Zechariah and
greeted Elizabeth" (Luke 1:39–40).

Filled with the Holy Spirit and bearing Jesus within her, Mary
hastened to visit her cousin, to share in their mutual joy and to
attend to Elizabeth's needs in the final months of her pregnancy.
What a beautiful illustration of a love that cannot be contained,
that is never stagnant. Authentic love, Christian love, is a river
of freshness that wells up within us and carries us out to others,
spilling over into a life of service. When we know Christ, when
we have intimacy with Him, we will see Him everywhere and be
drawn to Him in the face of the helpless, the suffering, and the poor.

Elizabeth was drawn to others. The time before she entered the
convent was spent not only in prayer but in its natural and necessary overflow: works of mercy. "Love of neighbor," the Catechism
tells us, "is inseparable from love for God" (1878). Elizabeth did
not love God just on paper or in prayer. She loved Him in people.
She responded to them and loved them because she loved Him.
There really is no other way to love.

The children of the hundreds of women working in the Dijon
tobacco factory were formed into a youth club, and Elizabeth would

watch the little girls. She made for her parish clothes that were sold for the missions, and she assisted in teaching and preparing the children for their First Communion, visiting households to invite them to send the children to catechism classes.

She also paid visits to the poor and the sick in her neighborhood, sharing hopeful words and blessing their souls as well as their bodies. "I admired her a great deal during visits to the poor," her friend Marie remembered. "She had a word of amiable welcome which opens up hearts: she attracted the children and knew how to speak to them. Even in the hostile families, she knew how to find the means of saying something about the good God and about duty."[62]

Elizabeth entered each house as a reflection of Christ Himself, and it was Christ within her who ministered to His people in their spiritual and material hunger, weaving into a single motion of love both the spiritual and corporal works of mercy, those "charitable actions by which we come to the aid of our neighbor in his spiritual and bodily necessities (cf. Isa. 58:6–7; Heb. 13:3)" (CCC 2447).

The Church gives us seven spiritual works of mercy:

1. Admonish the sinner.
2. Instruct the ignorant.
3. Counsel the doubtful.
4. Bear wrongs patiently.
5. Forgive offenses willingly.
6. Comfort the afflicted.
7. Pray for the living and the dead.

And the Church gives us seven corporal works of mercy:

1. Feed the hungry.
2. Give drink to the thirsty.
3. Clothe the naked.

---

[62] Mosley, *Elizabeth of the Trinity*, vol. 1, 117.

Works of Mercy

4. Shelter the homeless.
5. Visit the sick.
6. Visit the imprisoned.
7. Bury the dead.

Every single day, we are given ways to pour out the very mercy of God upon the world. How generous He is to allow us to participate in His work of saving souls and reconciling the world to Himself! And sometimes the opportunities are closer and more numerous than we realize: we may not have to look far to see where we are called to serve.

Several years ago, I was at a funeral Mass for a friend's mother, and my two youngest were with me. We lasted only a few minutes in the main church. My three-year-old, his toddler voice echoing during the quiet, solemn service, sent us into the vestibule. I could hear the readings from the speakers back there, and I listened while the kids sprawled at my feet. It was Matthew's Gospel of the Final Judgment, where Christ tells of separating the sheep from the goats. I felt my stomach knotting up as I listened.

> Then he will say to those at his left hand, "Depart from me, you cursed, into the eternal fire prepared for the devil and his angels; for I was hungry and you gave me no food, I was thirsty and you gave me no drink, I was a stranger and you did not welcome me, naked and you did not clothe me, sick and in prison and you did not visit me." (Matt. 25:41–43)

Ugh. It had been a long time since I had volunteered at a soup kitchen. Did making meals for a new mom count? Maybe not. Although, hey: there was that Gatorade I gave to a guy looking for change in the Costco parking lot. Hmmm ... I delivered some outgrown clothes to the parish rummage sale last month. Not quite the same as clothing the naked, though. I had never visited a prison either. Was leading a women's group instructing the ignorant? Not sure. This wasn't looking good. I hung my head, feeling very much like a goat.

And then, as if on cue, I felt a sticky hand tugging on my skirt. "Mommy, can I have some water? I'm thirsty."

I absently handed my son the water bottle, and then, as I looked at the little face, everything became clear. As if God Himself had adjusted the lens and put my life back into focus.

Truly, I say to you, as you did it to one of the least of these my brethren, you did it to me. (Matt. 25:40)

Of course. I knew then what the King was trying to tell me. This was the time in my life when the "least" were my little ones. (Although now some of my little ones are taller than their mother!) Six times I had welcomed tiny strangers to this new, bright world, clothed them in pink and blue hats and blankets, fed them, and nursed them through countless nights of fevers and tummy aches. Three times I had welcomed new life and had to give it back again before I could do any of those things.

And still now, all the grocery shopping, mac-and-cheese making, loading endless piles of socks and sheets and basketball jerseys into the washing machine, teaching them their prayers, taking them to Mass: in all these things, I was doing what God wanted me to do. I was taking care of Him, of Him living and dwelling in the souls of those He had deliberately entrusted to me.

Yes, I could do more. I should do more. I recalled singing Christmas carols with my kids at a nursing home and visiting elderly relatives on the weekends. We needed to do more of that as a family. But the reality is, I don't have a lot of time to take from this precious bunch of kids to put into outside service right now, in this particular season. It would be an injustice to take too much of what is theirs — my time and attention — and give it away.

Works of Mercy

For now, I had to be primarily a missionary into the heart of my family.

There are no shortages of quotes from Mother Teresa about this very reality. People would want to do what she did, to care for the poorest of the poor in the farthest corners of the earth. But she would always point them back to their own families first:

> Do you know the poor of your own home first? Maybe in your home there is somebody who is feeling lonely, very unwanted, very handicapped. Maybe your husband, your wife, or your child is lonely. Do you know that?[63]

Elizabeth knew it. She was always available and sensitive to her sister, her mother, her friends. Nursing her mother through a long illness, soothing with love and prayer her anxious heart, writing frequent letters to many during her convent years with promises to "meet" them in prayer in the presence of God: it was all so important to her. These were the precious souls God had put directly into her life to love. She never lost sight of that priority, even when separated from them. Our Lady, too, may have hurried to the hills when she was needed there, but she spent thirty years hidden at home serving her husband and her son.

And when we put others before ourselves, even—no, especially—when they are in our own homes, when we bring Christ into our kitchens and our shopping carts and our minivans and our arms and laps, we can be very sure of this: if you are caring for His lambs, you are one of the sheep.

---

[63] Mother Teresa of Calcutta, "God Has Sent the Family to Be His Love," *Co-Worker Newsletter*, no. 34 (Spring/Summer 1989). For the complete message, see Family Life Council, Inc., http://www.4life4family.org/mother-teresa-message/.

I demand from you deeds of mercy, which are to arise out of love for Me. You are to show mercy to your neighbors always and everywhere.

— St. Faustina, *Diary*, no. 742

Questions for Reflection

What are some works of mercy that you feel drawn to?

How can you put them into practice?

Is there anyone close to home who may need some extra time and attention right now?

15

Friends in Heaven

"Pray to St. Rita!" I posted on Facebook, along with a story of her life, on her feast day a few years ago. A friend, a kind-hearted Christian doctor who had seen me through my fifth pregnancy—and an elder in his large Bible church—left a comment: "May I suggest praying to the One True God?"

I paused, considering carefully how to answer. I knew this was a common misunderstanding with non-Catholics, and I saw it as an opportunity.

"Of course!" I replied. "But we have friends in heaven just as we have friends on earth. And our prayers for each other do not end with death."

The next day he added under my response: "1 Timothy 2:5."

I reached for my Bible and found the passage: "For there is one God and one mediator between God and men, the man Christ Jesus."

This time I didn't have to think. The Holy Spirit gave me the words immediately: "Yes, there is one Mediator, and it is Jesus Christ. But God in His goodness allows us to participate in that mediation—just as you, as a doctor, cannot heal by your own power but administer and share in the healing power of the One Divine Physician. This is what exactly happens when you pray for me and I pray for you." I thought of him praying with me before my daughter's birth.

He had no other reply, just a "love" on my comment, and our exchange ended. But I've thought of that often since. God really could answer all of our prayers on His own. But it is precisely because He loves us that He does not leave us as spectators to salvation, sitting on the sidelines. Instead, He allows us to get off the bench and into the game—to pray for each other, to fast and sacrifice for each other, to enter into each other's lives and longings and sufferings by entering into His own exchange of love with His Father. It's such a beautiful mystery. It is part of being in this glorious Body of Christ, the Church.

I've always found incredible inspiration and consolation from reading the lives of the saints—the players in the end zone but still very much on the team. I've had prayers answered with clear signs that it was through their pleading before the throne of God. And while we might turn to them for specific causes, looking for answers or even miracles, I often talk to them like friends and find them ready to accompany me even in the smallest and most insignificant parts of my day. They model what it means to be Christian in very specific ways. They show us what faith looks like lived out. They teach us to be truly ourselves.

"Follow the saints, because those who follow them will become saints," Pope St. Clement I tells us.[64]

St. Elizabeth of the Trinity believed that too. Her life and spirituality were very much shaped by her spiritual reading, certainly of Scripture but also the writings of saints, including the great Carmelite mystics St. Teresa of Avila and St. John of the Cross. These were the great reformers who had transformed the order centuries before, returning it to a more ascetic and cloistered life

---

[64] Pope St. Clement I, *Letter to the Corinthians*, chap. 46.

and deeper prayer: the very charisms that drew Elizabeth. She would come to love these saints, to see their prayer and interior experience reflected in hers.

Before she entered Carmel, she was given a book of writings by a woman who had yet to be named a saint, but whose mission had already taken off from heaven, as she had promised before her death: Thérèse of Lisieux. Thérèse had died only two years before, but her biography was creating quite a stir already, and it certainly stirred Elizabeth's heart. She recognized a kindred spirit in the little saint and her simple spirituality, and Thérèse's prayer of Oblation to Merciful Love so struck Elizabeth that she copied it several times and was inspired to make her own offering in November of 1899: "Make me a martyr of your love," she wrote.[65] The great gift of Thérèse, not only to her Carmelite sister Elizabeth but to all in the Dijon convent (and before long, to the world), was the blush of Divine Mercy over a horizon clouded with a harsher, more judgmental spirituality choking Catholic France at the time.

Elizabeth would not only embrace little Thérèse as her spiritual teacher but recommend her to others: she simply had to share her with those she loved. "I am entrusting you to a little Carmelite named Thérèse of the Child Jesus," she wrote to friends. "Her grace is to expand souls, to launch them on the waves of love, confidence, and abandonment.... Will you invoke her every day with me, so she can obtain for you the knowledge that makes saints and gives the soul so much peace and happiness?"[66]

Saint Thérèse herself had a deep appreciation for the communion of saints — whether in heaven or on earth. She knew that especially when the veil was torn apart in the earth-shattering

---

[65] Moorcroft, He Is My Heaven, 46.
[66] Letter 249, in Nash, Complete Works, vol. 2, 230.

celebration of the liturgy, there was nothing dividing us from those we loved and who had gone ahead of us—only our inability to see.

When Elizabeth entered Carmel, she filled out a questionnaire that asked for her favorite saints. St. Teresa of Avila and St. John the Apostle topped the list. Her retreat, "Heaven in Faith," begins with words of Jesus from John's Gospel: "Father, I will that where I am they also whom You have given Me may be with Me, in order that they may behold My glory which You have given Me, because You have loved Me before the creation of the world."

That where I am they also whom You have given Me may be with Me.

If we are with Christ, then we are together in Him. Elizabeth had a very deep awareness of our communion together, on earth, bound by Christ and one in Him, "our indissoluble bond." She knew that, whether or not we are together in place, we can be united in the heart of Jesus and that through Him we are not limited by time or space. "It seems to me," she wrote, "that the souls on earth and those glorified in the light of vision are so close to each other, since they are all in communion with the same God, the same Father, who gives Himself to the former in faith and mystery and satisfies the others in His divine light."[67]

"Prayer links souls together," she said, and she would make plans to "meet" her distant loved ones before the Eucharist or the Crucifix, sometimes settling on specific times for a spiritual rendezvous.

"Grilles, distance, time, nothing, it seems to me, will be able to separate our souls; for we love each other in God, and in Him, there is no separation!" She was confident of the invisible cords of union. To a friend who had just lost a baby, she wrote, "This whole invisible world draws near to us in the light of faith, and communion is established between those above and those below!"[68]

---

[67] Letter 124, in Nash, *Complete Works*, vol. 2, 53.
[68] Letter 142, in Nash, *Complete Works*, vol. 2, 73.

Friends in Heaven

Wouldn't it be natural, then, that after she died, she would desire to unite with those of us still making our way? Wouldn't her intercession increase, her love expand, her heart surge with the wish to draw us to know the love and power of the Trinity within our very hearts? To have what she has, to know what she knows, to love in the way she loves?

Is that not why I am writing this now, and you are reading it? Is this not some great unfolding story in which we — the characters — are closer than we know and the plot lines intersect at every turn?

We'll talk about Elizabeth's heavenly mission later. But for now, hold this thought: she knew very well what I shared with my doctor-friend:

We have friends in heaven just as we have friends on earth. And our prayers for each other do not end with death.

Questions for Reflection

Which saints are some of your favorites?

How have they influenced, instructed, or strengthened you?

How does the idea of the communion of saints inspire you?

16

I Will Restore the Years

I don't remember how I first came upon it, that little Scripture verse that snagged my heart. I wrote it down on an index card and hung it in the kitchen:

I will restore to you the years which the swarming locust has eaten. (Joel 2:25)

And I thought about it for a long time, the word "restoration" swelling in me, telling me things, inviting me to trust God, who has a plan for wholeness and rebuilding and resurrection.

But how, I wondered, does God restore years? I knew well how God could open up hours by multiplying moments: the tasks of the day mysteriously getting done even though morning Mass ran long, or the unexpected free afternoon when my spirit had been suffocated by too many commitments.

But years?

Does God have a time machine or a Rewind button? Well, He could if He wanted to. But what I've realized is that God does not restore years by fixing them or redoing them.

God restores years *by redeeming them.*

One summer, I discovered why God had given me that Scripture verse, telling me to save it for later. I spent several afternoons with

This Present Paradise

my daughter, rereading one of my favorite childhood books: *On the Banks of Plum Creek*, by Laura Ingalls Wilder. I hadn't opened that book in decades, and as my daughter and I read it together I felt a flood of memories as thick as the prairie grass. I remembered reading the story of the grasshopper summers as a little girl, but now, as an adult, it made me ache in a new, awful way—seeing it from the point of view of Laura's parents, who had staked their money and hopes and future on a bit of prairie land in Minnesota and built it all on credit and faith in their first wheat crop. And then, just when it was almost harvest time, they had to watch helplessly as a cloud of millions of giant brown grasshoppers descended out of nowhere and devoured every living plant in sight—including their wheat, the very stuff of their life and livelihood.

I imagined what it was to live and move and continue on, day after long day, with the once-green ground covered in grasshoppers, the sound of their endless eating in their ears and crunching under their feet, the sound of their future being chewed away by an Old Testament plague come back to test every last ounce of their hope.

> There was no rain, and the days went by, hotter and hotter, uglier and uglier, and filled with the sound of grasshoppers until it seemed that no more could be borne.
>
> "Oh, Charles," Ma said one morning, "seems to me I can't bear one more day of this."
>
> Ma was sick. Her voice was white and thin, and she sat down tired as she spoke.
>
> Pa did not answer. For days he had been going out and coming in with a still, tight face. He did not sing or whistle any more. It was worst of all when he did not answer Ma. He walked to the door and stood looking out.[69]

---

[69] Laura Ingalls Wilder, *On the Banks of Plum Creek* (New York: Harper & Row, 1971), 261–262.

I Will Restore the Years

And then, in the second year of this suffering, this original-sin, cursed-ground and toil and dust and sweat kind of suffering, the grasshoppers simply left. They marched west for days and finally flew off, with their backs to the eastern horizon—where we have always watched for the first sign of our salvation.

> Ma went into the house and threw herself down in a rocking-chair. "My Lord!" she said. "My Lord!" The words were praying, but they sounded like, "Thank you!"[70]

Were those lost years? They were eaten years, gnawed years, devoured years. But in the end, they were restored years. They were restored because the harvest was in maturing hearts and spiritual fruitfulness, years restored to wholeness by a surrendered kind of suffering that gave a family strength out of devastation and would inspire millions of readers for generations—including one particular middle-aged mom weeping over it on a summer afternoon. Laura brought me into those broken years, and I came out and suddenly understood this with clarity: *I will restore to you the years*.

And so it was with Elizabeth. There were those five years of waiting when her mother's hesitancy and possessiveness ate away at a young life, a life that would be far too short in the end. Years of fresh wheat, a week away from harvest, mowed down and left out by indecision.

How did God restore her lost years, her waiting years? By redeeming every not-yet moment, washing it in His blood, and hanging it out on the line of her life for us to see; by inspiring us as we read of a loving, longing girl growing into a surrendered woman who was finding a pure kind of faith. We learn from her as we see her pray during the wait, her prayer becoming simplified and more perfect. We watch her crawl deeper into herself and find Jesus

[70] Ibid., 266.

there — and make it her very mission to help us do the same. Yes, those years were very much restored. And we are still gathering grain from her "devoured" years.

God will restore our years too. What gnawed or enemy-eaten past can we give back to a God, who wants nothing for us but wholeness?

God will wrap them up in His mercy and bind them back up into a life of completeness that glories Him because of the disappointing and bitten-off pieces, not in spite of them.

Prayer to Redeem Lost Time, by St. Teresa of Avila

O my God! Source of all mercy!
I acknowledge Your sovereign power.
While recalling the wasted years that are past,
I believe that You, Lord, can in an instant
turn this loss to gain.
Miserable as I am, yet I firmly believe that
You can do all things.
Please restore to me the time lost,
giving me Your grace,
both now and in the future,
that I may appear before You
in "wedding garments."
Amen.

Questions for Reflection

What years can you give to God to restore?

Do you trust that God can and will restore them?

How has the Lord redeemed any
brokenness in your past?

17

To Have Eternal Life

Finally.

At the age of twenty-one, Elizabeth turned toward the convent, at last open to her, as her mother had promised. The last weeks before her entrance on August 2, 1901, were full of intense emotion and many goodbyes, visits, and farewell letters. And then, suddenly, there it was: the last dinner, the last evening in her home. The night before she was to enter, her mother came into her room and knelt by her bed, overcome with grief. Even as they cried together, Elizabeth told her that she simply had to respond to the call of her Beloved, who had finally said: *It is time.*

In the Gospel, Jesus had just watched the rich young man walk sadly away, unable to leave everything in order to follow Him, when Peter spoke up, reminding the Lord that the Twelve had given up everything to be His disciples. Jesus looked at the fisherman without nets, without a boat, without a livelihood. He looked at James and John, who had walked away even while their father watched, wondering, from the lonely shore. And knowing that they were just the first of many who would make hard, hard decisions, who would sever ties and say goodbyes and with twisted stomachs and broken hearts leave good things for better ones, He said this:

This Present Paradise

And every one who has left houses or brothers or sisters or father or mother or children or lands, for my name's sake, will receive a hundredfold, and inherit eternal life. (Matt. 19:29)

The convent was right around the corner but it was a world away, literally: it was removed from the world so that its community could pray for the world; it was set apart to extend the prayer of Jesus—that in Him all would be one (John 17:21). But such single-hearted unity requires a radical slicing away of everything else. Isn't such a contradiction typical of the Christian life? Death is life, loss is gain, to be last is to be first. Nothing is as it seems. And so Elizabeth left her family and her friends in order to be, with Christ, totally for them.

Just hours before she left her home for the last time, Elizabeth wrote to Canon Angles, the priest who had received her secret, whispered wish so many years ago: "I want to be a nun!" Now he would unfold her letter to read:

> I love my mother as I have never loved her, and at the moment of consummating the sacrifice which will separate me from these two beloved creatures who are so good and whom He has chosen for me if you knew what peace is flooding my soul! I am no longer on earth, I feel that I am all His, that I am keeping nothing for myself, I am throwing myself into His arms like a little child.[71]

And so she left that morning with her mother, her sister, and a few friends for one final Mass at the convent chapel together. Afterward, the door to the enclosure opened, and Elizabeth walked in alone. She had heard Jesus say, *Follow me*, and now she joined that group of fishermen who stood with Him in Judea, empty-handed and yet set to inherit all the promises.

---

[71] Letter 81, in Mosley, *Elizabeth of the Trinity*, vol. 1, 160.

To Have Eternal Life

As her mother and sister walked slowly home, supported by their closest friends, they too — whether they knew it or not — were being covered in grace. It had been a hard, wrenching thing, this giving away of someone so lovely inside and out, who had become so steady, so loyal, so full of God. But what does He ever take away without giving more in return? The ones behind, the ones who watch from the shore — they are not forgotten, either. They make a sacrifice too; they still have to face the world, but they face it now a little more alone. Elizabeth was sensitive to this.

"Oh! If you knew how much I love you," she wrote a week later to her mother. "It seems to me that I will never be able to thank you enough for letting me enter this dear Carmel where I am so happy. It's partly to you that I owe my happiness, for you surely know that if you had not said 'yes,' your little Sabeth would have stayed close by you. Oh! My little mother, how the good God loves you, if you could see what tenderness He looks on you!"[72]

I imagine her mother, hands shaking, reading and rereading the familiar handwriting — trying to be happy. But sacrifice is always hard, or it is not a sacrifice. "What should I give up for Lent?" my children asked this year, wondering if they could give up candy — but not chocolate. I met their gaze, and they knew. It's not Lent if it is not difficult. It's not really living if it is not hard. There is a great severing at the end of life, and each little death is a practice for the one that really counts.

We all find ourselves at one time or another kneeling before the Good Master, eager and full of hope and joy and wanting to follow Him, only to realize that we are held back by something to which we've tethered ourselves. And there comes the moment — terrible and yet beautiful and the one we were created for — the moment we must slice the string, drop the nets, and choose Christ.

[72] Letter 85, in Nash, *Complete Works*, vol. 2, 10.

This Present Paradise

Questions for Reflection

Have you ever made a tremendous
sacrifice for love of God?

How did He sustain you?

What might God want you to release your grasp of?

18

And I Know You by Name

Our names. They are among the earliest sounds we recognize as babies and among the first things we write in scrawling letters as children. They are part of who we are; our names shape our identity and have such significance that just hearing someone's name calls to mind a whole person—character, appearance, history, and heart. We hope, too, that when the Book of Life is opened and read at the end of time, our names will be included in it. When God calls us, He does not call us in a general sense. He uses our names. He calls us by name.

To know someone's name, to call that person by name, holds a certain intimacy and even power many layers deep. Naming creation is one of the privileges God allows Adam as a participation in His creative work in the Garden of Eden. That is a tremendous responsibility and one that reveals Adam's headship. Only one name is not to be spoken outright in the Old Testament: the name of God.

Judeo-Christian tradition confirms that a person's name has a deep and lasting significance. In the Bible, a name tells us something of a person: "Adam" derives from a word meaning "ground" in Hebrew—a reference to the clay of which he was formed. David, the most loved king in the Old Testament, has a name that means "beloved." St. Joseph is given the profound honor of bestowing the chosen name for the Savior of the world: Jesus, which has as its root "to rescue or deliver." *You shall call his name Jesus, for he will save his people from their sins* (Matt. 1:21).

And so, as parents, we scour books full of the meanings and origins of thousands of baby names, letting the sounds roll off our tongues. We consider favorite family members and patron saints. Maybe we study obscure saints. We want something unique, yes, but not *too* unique. We weigh middle names and first names, stringing them together in different combinations. We shake our spouse awake at night with a brilliant idea for a name. Sometimes it seems that God had a particular name in mind all along, and we merely uncovered it.

The LORD called me from the womb, from the body of my mother *he named my name.*

—Isaiah 49:1

"Daniel and Elizabeth, what name do you give your child?" Cradling their first baby, my parents answered confidently, "Claire Elizabeth."

I would learn later that the Franciscan charism—poverty, simplicity, charity—had already laid hold of their hearts. Their first date, in fact, had been to see a movie about St. Francis and St. Clare. So the name Claire had been a natural choice, and then Elizabeth, was, of course, after my mom—although I have a strong suspicion that a certain St. Elizabeth in heaven may have been whispering in their ears too.

I've come to appreciate that "Claire" comes from the Latin word meaning "light" or "clear"—something I've always tried to be in speaking and in writing.

And I Know You by Name

My identity would take on another layer when "Anne"—after the saint, and meaning "grace"—was spoken over the chrism cross on my forehead at my Confirmation, and when I married, I would joyfully take on my husband's last name as a sign of the great shift in my spiritual reality—for the fact was, I was no longer the same.

From Abraham and Sarah to Paul and Peter, new names are bestowed by God to signify a person's new role in salvation history. It is as if God says: *Pay close attention here. Something new is happening.*

Similarly, religious are often given new names as a sign of their new life when they join an order, marking a sacred beginning, a day of a being re-created and set apart for a divine purpose. A religious name is "something that articulates the spirituality of your heart, how you've received God and how you want to be a channel of His love," explained a religious friend of mine.

A Poor Clare of Perpetual Adoration shared with me her anticipation of and joy in receiving her brand-new religious name, which was revealed to her at the investiture ceremony by her abbess, Mother Angelica:

> In many orders, the investiture ceremony is private and takes place in the community's chapter room. But, at that time, Mother Angelica chose to have our investiture ceremonies directly follow Mass so that they could be televised on EWTN. Not only were our family and friends present in the Chapel, but so many others were able to take part in the joy via television!
>
> After I received the habit, Mother stood before me with the parchment scroll on which was written my new name. It was a nerve-racking, thrilling, and soul-stirring moment. With her commanding voice, both strong and full of affection, Mother said: "In order to begin your life with Jesus, you will no longer be known by your baptismal name. You

will be called by a new name, one which the mouth of the Lord will confer." I was then given my new religious name and title.

I asked her, "Were you happy with it or did it have to grow on you?"

"YES!" She shared. "I loved it. Immediately."

She explained how it was chosen:

Customs vary from order to order. In some orders, sisters choose their own name. For us, though, we are allowed to submit three names. After much prayer, the abbess picks one of them or another of her choosing. A few months before my investiture, Mother told me that she had chosen my name even though I had yet to submit the three names I desired. All the same, she asked me to submit my choices. Providentially, I had put for my first choice what Mother Angelica had chosen for me! Over time in many varied ways, God would reveal its perfection, through a deepening sense of both mission and identity.[73]

As a child, Elizabeth Catez was delighted when she was told her name meant "House of God." It confirmed her inner experience of God dwelling within her soul, communicating Himself to her, buried within her. She would meditate deeply on that reality, and she knew even as a child that it held a significance for her.

When Elizabeth was to enter the Carmelites, she had hoped to be "Sr. Elizabeth of Jesus" because of her deep devotion to Christ crucified. The Mother Superior, Mother Marie of Jesus, revealed instead that she was to be dedicated to the Most Holy Trinity: *Sr. Marie Elizabeth of the Trinity*. Elizabeth had to surrender her first

---

[73] Sr. Mary Fidelis, PCPA, in an e-mail exchange with the author, April 2020.

choice, but she came to love her new name and all that it signified: the reality of the unity of the Father, Son, and Holy Spirit. Deep within this mystery, her charism was uncovered. Her name was a sort of seal on her mission. "It seems to me this name signifies a particular vocation, isn't that beautiful? I so love this mystery of the Holy Trinity, it is an abyss in which I lose myself."[74] "I am still called Elizabeth," she wrote, "but I also bear the name of the Holy Trinity. *Sr. Elizabeth of the Trinity*. Isn't that a beautiful name?"[75] (In 1932, Guite's oldest daughter would enter the same convent and receive the name her aunt had originally wanted: *Sr. Elizabeth of Jesus*. How beautifully God brings everything full circle sometimes!)

"In the (Carmelite) order, the title incorporated into one's name indicates that God wishes to bind the soul to himself under the sign of a particular mystery of faith," explains St. Edith Stein. She mentions that, in the case of St. John of the Cross, "by changing his name, John showed that the cross was superimposed on his life as an emblem."[76] So "of the Trinity" was no mere afterthought. It was deeply, supernaturally significant.

From the beginning, before Mother Marie knew, before Elizabeth knew, *God knew*. He knew Elizabeth, and he knew her by name.

Perhaps there is a symbol, a mission, a meaning, or a heavenly connection woven into your name too. What treasure is buried beneath those syllables? You may not yet know, but you can know this: God knows. He has always known your name, and He knows your full identity in Him. Ask Him to show you.

---

[74] Letter 62, in Mosley, *Elizabeth of the Trinity*, vol. 1, 142.
[75] Letter 136, in Nash, *Complete Works*, vol. 2, 72.
[76] Edith Stein, *The Science of the Cross* (Washington, DC: ICS Publications, 2002), 9.

This Present Paradise

You have found favor in my sight,
and I know you by name.

— Exodus 33:17

Questions for Reflection

Do you know the meaning or
significance behind your name?

Do you see any connection between your
name and your mission or spirituality?

Have you ever asked God to reveal
a deeper meaning to you?

If you are a parent, how did you
choose your children's names?

19

What Is Your Motto?

The week Elizabeth entered the convent in August of 1901, she was handed a questionnaire. Whenever time allowed in those early, busy days, she would jot down her replies to questions about her most-loved saints (St. Teresa of Avila and St. John, the beloved disciple), her favorite virtue (purity), and her favorite part of the rule (silence). She shared what name she'd like to have in heaven (The will of God) and her motto (God in me, I in Him).

God in me, I in Him: an insight into the interplay between the soul and her Beloved, moving and living — a relationship, deep and dynamic. These six simple words summarize Elizabeth's spirituality. In a sense, everything she would write and say and do over the next five years would develop from this one idea. "God in me, I in Him," she wrote in a letter to Canon Angles before her entrance. "Oh! That is my life!"[77]

This is an ancient tradition in the Church: saints, bishops, and religious orders have long taken mottos to guide their spiritualities, decisions, and actions. The Discalced Carmelite order has its own motto: "With zeal have I been zealous for the Lord; God of hosts" — the words of the prophet Elijah before the Lord God spoke

[77] Letter 62, in Mosley, *Elizabeth of the Trinity*, vol. 1, 141.

to him in a still, small voice. The Jesuits have a famous one: *Ad maiorem Dei gloriam*, "For the greater glory of God," and, in that tradition, my little first grader marks the top of his school papers with a scrawling "AMDG."

The Franciscans live by the words *Pax et bonum*, "Peace and the good." The Dominicans motto, encircling their coat of arms, reads, *Audare, benedicere, praedicare*, "to praise, to bless, to preach."

Members of my religious community of Apostoli Viae take to heart *Unum est Necessarium*, the words of Jesus directed to the busy Martha as Mary sat at His feet: "One thing," he said, "is necessary" (see Luke 10:42).

Bishop Thomas Olmsted, the shepherd of my diocese of Phoenix, has taken the motto "Jesus Caritas," or "Love of Jesus," which he personifies every day. Pope St. John Paul II's was simple but famous: "Totus Tuus," or "Totally yours," referring to his total entrustment to Our Lady. St. John Henry Newman's is also well known: "Heart speaks to heart."

I've always loved the idea of a personal motto, and I had thought about mine for years, mulling it over and wondering if there was a verse or a word that could sum up my heart and my calling—and one night it came to me, just like that. I sat up in bed, bleary-eyed, and scribbled it down. It was a direct download from the Holy Spirit.

The words were these: *Respect Life, Reveal Truth, Radiate Love.*

A threefold mission blazoned on my heart that night and would become my motto, so to speak—a commission, revealing itself more and more each day, and a compass, too, by which I can set a course or check my trajectory. When I have to make a choice about an action or an opportunity or a direction, big or small, I hold it up to those few words. How well do they align?

For St. Elizabeth of the Trinity, "God in me, I in Him," would take on layer-upon-layer of meaning as she came to understand how true it was: in her prayer, in her experiences, in her long, dark nights and unifying sufferings. She would go to great lengths to explain it to her loved ones in letters so rich in a lived theology that we still are learning from them today.

Have you ever thought about crafting a simple sentence that could sum up your calling, even if it is just for a particular season — something to help keep you single-hearted, clear, and deliberate in how you live and love and pray? It could be a verse or a phrase from the Bible. It could be pulled from a quote of a patron saint or represent a cause you've been called to. Try sitting with it awhile. Often, I think, the answer comes when you are least expecting it.

But the question itself is like an invitation to God to speak a few words of deep meaning over your life, to reveal something about you: when He knit you together, He wove some words in your soul — echoes of the one, eternal Word.

Whether or not you hold an office or a title or can claim a religious community, you have a purpose and were created with a call. You carry a particular part of the Gospel into the world. Claim it; invite God into it. And consider, what is your motto?

Questions for Reflection

Do you live by a standard or idea that
you could craft into a motto?

Do you know the motto of your parish,
school, community, or patron saint?

Do you think having a motto could help
you "set a course" in your spiritual life?

20

The Life of a Carmelite

My friend Katherine and I walked hesitantly up to the door, on which hung a sign inviting visitors into the small lobby of the cloistered Carmelite convent in Alhambra, California. We slipped into the quiet and waited, glancing curiously about the simple interior. In front of us was a stairway, to our left a small parlor with a screen to separate nuns from visitors, and to our right a closed door. After a moment of silence and uncertainty, Katherine nudged me and pointed to a small opening in the wall opposite us.

A tiny window began to turn with a soft grating sound. We heard a barely audible whisper and crept toward it. "Hello ..." It sounded like a voice from another world, a breeze from Mount Horeb which required absolute stillness to hear: "Can I help you?"

We bent over the screen and explained that we were about to begin a retreat for women the following day and would be grateful for the community's prayers for all involved. We were assured in hushed tones that the nuns would be praying for us.

I had a sudden inspiration. "May we stay and pray here awhile?" I asked, imagining us kneeling right there in the lobby.

"Would you like to pray in our chapel?" The muffled voice asked. We looked at each other.

Chapel?

This Present Paradise

To our right, we heard the sound of a buzzer and a door unlock-
ing. We pushed the door open and entered a beautiful sanctuary
full of filtered light and a hundred years of prayer. I could see the
grille behind which the nuns prayed. As we knelt, I honestly felt
that I was somewhere utterly timeless and yet completely rooted.

What tradition were we tiptoeing into? It was the same cen-
turies-old spiritual space occupied by St. Elizabeth of the Trinity
and the thousands like her who had chosen a life of hiddenness
and obscurity and openness to grace. It was an inheritance of silence and solitude and perpetual prayer, of praise and reparation
and intercession behind walls and screens and grilles—not to be
a prison, but rather a sanctuary for something invaluable. "The
more precious the love, the more precautions to guard it," wrote
Archbishop Fulton Sheen. "The grating in a Carmelite monastery
is not to keep the sisters in, but to keep the world out."[78]

The first Carmelites were pilgrims or crusaders who stayed in
the Holy Land and lived hidden away in little cells on Mount
Carmel, like the prophet Elijah, their spiritual father. Their austere
rule was written by St. Albert, the patriarch of Jerusalem, in the
early 1200s. When the Holy Land fell to the Muslims and became
unsafe, the early monks left to set up monasteries around Europe.
The Carmelites became one of the four great mendicant orders,
meaning that the intentional personal and communal poverty of
the order necessitated begging for basic needs.

The first community of nuns was founded in that penitential
spirit of poverty in 1452. But just over a hundred years later, St.
Teresa of Avila began to realize, in the midst of her deeper conversion, that the order had fallen away from the strictness of its
founding charism. She wanted to do away with visitors in the

[78] Fulton J. Sheen, *The World's First Love* (San Francisco: Ignatius
Press, 1996), 167.

convents, frivolous conversations, nuns' owning personal property, and other distractions and abuses. Together with St. John of the Cross, she began a reform to bring back the order's foundational sacred simplicity, and the Discalced ("shoeless," in reference to the sandals they wore) Carmelites were born.

The Convent in Dijon, into which Elizabeth Catez had happily disappeared to become Sr. Elizabeth of the Trinity, was a Discalced Carmelite convent founded in 1605, about twenty years after the death of St. Teresa of Avila. The nuns in Dijon fully embraced the deep spirit of prayer of their foundress, and it was that life of asceticism and self-giving that enchanted Elizabeth. It was a perfect place for her to bloom — a flower in the arid but beautiful desert of Carmel.

There she would live fully a life of liturgical prayer, days and weeks and years regulated by the rhythm of the Church, connecting the sisters to the seasons of heaven. When writing about their celebration of the Immaculate Conception in 1904, Elizabeth confided, "It was like an echo of the heavenly feast."[79] The Liturgy of the Hours was like the pulse of their community, offered at regular intervals between personal prayer, communal meals, and the discipline of daily work.

In a letter, Elizabeth describes her day:

> We begin our day with an hour of prayer at 5 o'clock in the morning, then we spend another hour in choir to say the Divine Office ... then Mass. At 2 p.m. we have Vespers, at 5 p.m. prayer until 6 p.m. At 7:45, Compline. Then we pray until Matins, which is said at 9 p.m., and it is only around 11 p.m. that we leave the choir to go to take our rest. During the day we have two hours of recreation; then, after that,

---

[79] Letter 216, in Nash, *Complete Works*, vol. 2, 183.

silence the whole time. When I am not sweeping, I work
in our little cell.[80]

Elizabeth, at the time of this letter, was a "habit sister," who assisted
with mending the nuns' habits during work hours.

Such a regulated life, but so desired by our saint: she saw that by
burying herself without distraction in prayer and in the Church's
deepest vocation, love itself, she was becoming totally available
not only to God but to the entire world. The apparent limitations
and exactness of the rule existed so that she could conquer herself,
or rather, maybe, be conquered by Christ, and therefore be empty
and ready to serve. So, in the end, the rule gives absolute freedom
and complete peace.

"How freeing it is!" wrote my friends the Poor Clares about
their rule, or *horarium*, as they call it. "How it offers stable support
so as not to squander time and turn in on ourselves. It provides
structure to our day that naturally lends itself to prayer, healthy
habits, creative outlets, and authentically human (life-giving) expe-
rience/encounters (like consistently sharing meals and meaningful
conversation), enjoying both communal (familial) and personal
(quiet) times of recreation."

My friend Christina has given the Church her oldest daughter
as a Dominican novice. As difficult as the separation and surrender is, Christina shared with me something her Annie (now Sr.
Catherine Paul) said in a moment of insight and profound truth as
she prepared to leave: "I'll never have to wonder if I'm doing the
will of God again." Suddenly, in that light, the humility of obedience and the docility to the rule of an order become so clearly and
totally releasing. Within it, what appears to be rigid and constrain-
ing — whether it be the rule or the will of the superiors — actually

---

[80] Letter 168, in Nash, *Complete Works*, vol. 2, 108.

sets one completely at liberty to serve without wasting a moment wondering what that service should look like. The contemplative nun rises in the morning to pray and work and obey and die a little more to herself, to offer herself for the Church with all the missionary zeal of the apostles and martyrs and in total union with them. And not one moment or ounce of her strength is wasted or dissipated.

"From what troubles we are saved, my God, by the vow of obedience!" exclaimed St. Thérèse. "The simple religious, guided by the will of her superiors alone, has the joy of being sure that she is on the right path; even when she is sure that her Superiors are mistaken, she need not fear."[81]

For me, who sometimes wanders around wondering what in the world I should do next, overwhelmed by the sheer volume of choices and the crush of daily responsibilities, this breathes a certain appeal. And so, while I don't have superiors (save the mutual surrender in marriage), I too have a simple—a very simple—rule to guide my days: basic prayer, family needs and obligations, set time for work, and even a bit of reading penciled in. When I know that there's a time for everything, the one thing necessary is never neglected and each next right thing—whether it is a hungry child or a messy kitchen—can have my full attention.

"It will be an essential duty of each individual to consider how she must shape her plan for daily and yearly living, according to her bent and respective circumstances of life, in order to make ready the way for the Lord," taught St. Edith Stein while she was living as a professional woman in her years before she entered the convent. "The exterior allotment must be different for each one, and it must also adjust resiliently to the change of circumstances in

[81] *The Story of a Soul*, 124.

the course of time," she added. [82] In other words, a rule, created for my precise vocation and season of life doesn't just save my sanity: it may save my soul.

St. Elizabeth would agree: "From morning to evening the Rule is there to express the will of God, moment by moment. If you knew how I love this Rule, which is *the way He wants me to become holy* ..."[83]

That's what it is, I thought while kneeling in that Carmelite chapel in California, breathing in air, which was mingled with incense and sanctity. That something that is firmly grounded in the now and yet seems to surpass it somehow. It is simply this: holiness.

Let us know how to prove our love to God by fidelity to our holy Rule; let us have a holy passion for it; if we keep it, it will keep us and make us saints.[84]

—St. Elizabeth of the Trinity

Questions for Reflection

If you live by a rule of life, how has it helped you focus on what is most important?

If not, do you feel called to create one?

What would you incorporate into it?

[82] Stein, *Essays on Woman*, 145, emphasis mine.
[83] Letter 168, in Nash, *Complete Works*, vol. 2, 108.
[84] Letter 299, in Nash, *Complete Works*, vol. 2, 309.

21

Faith or Feelings

When Elizabeth stepped into the convent and entered into religious life as a postulant, she left behind her close-knit family, friends and confidants, stylish clothes, fashionable hairstyles, accomplished piano-playing, and scenic summer vacations. She gave up the entire world and slipped into a simple dark dress and veil and began to dissolve into Carmel. And she couldn't have been happier. So many long-held desires were finally fulfilled, and she was not disappointed as her dreams became her daily life.

The separation itself was difficult, but her joy was immense. For months, she was flooded with light. The Lord had led her to Himself and allowed her to feel His presence and unspeakable tenderness. The veil between them was almost transparent.

"I have found what I was searching for," she said to her sister. "Oh my darling, how good God is!" [85]

Everything, no matter how menial, felt divine: "Since you like me to tell you lots of things, here is something very interesting: we've done the wash. For the occasion I put on my nightcap, my brown dress all turned up, a large apron over that, and, to complete the outfit, our wooden shoes. I went down to the laundry room

---

[85] Letter 86, in Nash, *Complete Works*, vol. 2, 11.

where they were scrubbing for all they were worth, and I tried to do like the others. I splashed and soaked myself all over, but that didn't matter, I was thrilled! Oh, you see, everything is delightful in Carmel, we find God at the wash just as at prayer. Everywhere there is only Him. We live Him, breathe Him. If you knew how happy I am, my horizon grows larger each day."[86]

So conscious was she of God's love that nothing on the outside could touch her, and everything tasted of God. "We find Him in our sleep just as we do in prayer since He is in everything, everywhere, and always!"[87]

This blissful state is called "consolation," and as Dan Burke explains in his book *Spiritual Warfare and the Discernment of Spirits*, it is "an interior movement to God, toward faith, hope, and love, that is caused by the good spirits." When we are in consolation, he points out that we may experience:
- an increase of hope, or faith, or love, or all three
- my heart inflamed with love of God and goodness
- shedding of tears for love of God, sorrow for my sins, or gratitude
- a clear draw to heavenly things
- quiet and peace in the Lord[88]

These tangible times are sacred for a soul. These are the harvest times, the storehouse-filling times, the soak-it-up-and-savor-it times, when God is around every corner, palpable and able to be touched; when you close your eyes to pray and make immediate contact. You can feel Him everywhere, flooding into every crevice of your thirsty soul. And you drink—deeply.

---

[86] Letter 89, in Nash, *Complete Works*, vol. 2, 16–17.
[87] Letter 111, Ibid., 42.
[88] Dan Burke, *Spiritual Warfare and the Discernment of Spirits* (Manchester, NH: Sophia Institute Press, 2019), 45-46.

Faith or Feelings

The well was full for the entire time of her postulancy, about four months, and continued to bubble over through the clothing ceremony, which marked her transition to a novice. This "betrothal" ceremony is a beautiful tradition: the bride of Christ wears a wedding dress before receiving the habit, her forever sign of being set apart for Him.

For Elizabeth, it took place on December 8, 1901 — the feast of the Immaculate Conception and four years to the day after she had laid down her will and accepted God's, even if it meant she must give up Carmel forever. Her mother and Guite were there, along with some friends, one of whom led her down the aisle, since she had long ago lost her father and grandfathers. At the point in the ceremony when she received the habit, she seemed utterly carried away with emotion, swept up into the foyer of heaven. She appeared unaware of everyone around her.

But feelings like these are, in the end, just feelings. They are a gift, but they cannot last: they must give way in order for us to grow in the holy virtue of faith. Faith is an entirely free gift of God, but it is something to be asked for, assented to, nourished, and practiced. Or else we can find ourselves "shipwrecked" (see 1 Tim. 1:19).

Elizabeth came down from her spiritual high, and she came down hard. It began immediately after the ceremony as a period of dryness, commonly called "aridity." In these desert times, prayer feels like sand in the mouth, a searching for a bit of water, usually coming up empty. Living in the Southwest, I can think of it as the expanses of desolate emptiness, just a few resilient, scraggly shrubs popping up miraculously out of bone-dry crevices; of hot breezes that bake you like clay into something almost lifeless.

In those times, you have to hang on to belief like a piece of driftwood floating by in the shipwreck of your feelings. You must cling to your knowledge that God is unchanging — that the same Father who watered you with joy and peace and a deep sense of His love is the same yesterday, today, and forever, regardless of whether you feel Him and experience Him that way. You must give God a pure love that is completely removed from how you feel, even when the veil darkens into a heavy iron curtain.

St. Teresa of Avila compared experiencing dryness in prayer to a gardener lowering a bucket down into a well, over and over, and coming up empty every time until his arms ache. But his efforts, without any visible reward, greatly please the Master of the garden. "For the Master has confidence in the gardener because He sees that without any pay he is so very careful about what he was told to do. This gardener helps Christ carry the cross and reflects that the Lord lived with it all during His life. He doesn't desire the Lord's kingdom here below or ever abandon prayer. And so he is determined, even though this dryness may last for his whole life, not to let Christ fall with the cross."[89]

"Nothing should keep you from going to Him. Don't pay too much attention to whether you are fervent or discouraged; it is the law of our exile to pass from one state to the other like that. Believe that He never changes, that in His goodness He is always bending over you to carry you away and keep you safe in Him,"[90] Elizabeth was able to reflect later. Before she died, her language was even stronger: "What does it matter to the soul ... whether it feels or does not feel, whether it is in darkness or light, whether it enjoys or does not enjoy. It feels a kind of embarrassment in making any distinction between these things; and when it still feels affected by them, it holds itself in deep contempt for its lack of love and quickly looks to its Master that He might set it free."[91]

---

[89] St. Teresa of Avila, *The Book of Her Life*, 11.
[90] Letter 249, in Nash, *Complete Works*, vol. 2, 230.
[91] "Last Retreat," 145.

Faith or Feelings

Fundamental to babies' cognitive growth is their learning, through experience and development, the concept of object permanence: the fact that something they cannot see still exists and is not dependent on their perception of it. A baby comes to understand that Daddy, who has walked through the door, has not disappeared but is in the other room, and he crawls eagerly after to find him.

Likewise, we may not realize that in our spiritual scan of the barren horizon, God is leading us farther up the mountain to Him, while He remains just out of reach. It feels futile and dusty. But we can make out footprints, and with grace, we keep climbing.

O my God, let me never forget that seasons of
consolation are refreshments here, and nothing more;
not our abiding state. They will not remain with
us, except in heaven. Here they are only intended
to prepare us for doing and suffering. I pray Thee,
O my God, to give them to me from time to time.
Shed over me the sweetness of Thy Presence, lest I
faint by the way.... Give me Thy Divine consolations
from time to time; but let me not rest in them.
Let me use them for the purpose for which Thou
givest them. Let me not think it grievous, let me
not be downcast, if they go. Let them carry me
forward to the thought and the desire of heaven.[92]

— St. John Henry Newman

---

[92] John Henry Newman, *Prayers, Poems, Meditations* (New York: Crossroad, 1990), 56.

We can thank God for this experience of Elizabeth's because it began a new understanding in her that would develop over the following years and even become one of her major works: "Heaven in Faith." The "heaven" she experienced in her spiritual high now took on a different dimension: heaven was still there, but it was held by faith. "The secret of happiness," she wrote to her sister while in this desert, "consists in union, in love! ... No longer being anything but 'one' with Him, that is to have one's Heaven in faith while awaiting the vision face to face!"[93]

In other words, one could still be united to God, but in this life, it is a union that must be grasped purely by belief, without seeing. And by holding on to faith, the muscles of our soul develop strength and stamina—something God knew she would need in the coming year.

These times can be trying, honestly, when prayer leaves you thirstier than before, when you white-knuckle it through. Yet they are necessary. "I love you too much to give you candy for breakfast," I've been known to say to a hungry child who has been caught sticky-fingered, rummaging for marshmallows in the kitchen as I brew my coffee. What he needs is oatmeal. Not as tasty, but far more filling.

And that's exactly it. When the desert sky opens and rain pours over parched hearts, we will stand slack-jawed at the sudden blooms, which had been sustained by secret, unseen wells within all along.

Blessed are those who have not seen and yet believe.

—John 20:29

---

[93] Letter 104, in Nash, *Complete Works*, vol. 2, 34–35.

Faith or Feelings

Questions for Reflection

Have you experienced periods of aridity?

Can you look back on them as something
necessary in the spiritual life — or
even as a blessing? In what way?

22

A Divine Darkness

The visiting American priest bowed his head in prayer before the Blessed Sacrament at the Mother House of the Missionaries of Charity in Calcutta. Suddenly, there was a gentle rustling at his side, and a sister pressed a note into his hand. He unfolded it to see Mother Teresa's handwriting:

Father,
please pray for me —
Where is Jesus?

Glancing at the tiny nun across the room, he met her intense gaze for the briefest of moments before she turned again to the Blessed Sacrament on the altar.[94]

It was a glimpse into a vast torrent of pain that the world would never know until St. Teresa's letters were made public after her death, a momentary window looking into an astonishing darkness that seemed, on the surface, to be nothing but light.

Her writings would expose decades of darkness, startling all of us who assumed — wrongly — that under her luminous simplicity and

---

[94] Paul Murray, *I Loved Jesus in the Night: Teresa of Calcutta: A Secret Revealed* (Brewster, MA: Paraclete Press, 2008) 48–49.

peaceful, beloved face lived a soul steeped in consolations. What else could move a woman to spend her life serving the poorest of the poor in the most wretched conditions? And yet now we know that she lived in a near-continuous state of total emptiness and bewildering abandonment. Heaving her heart, again and again, before the Lord in an excruciating state of surrender, trust, and faith, desiring deeply contact with the One who had for so long fallen silent within her.

The woman who seemed to be a living embodiment of the love of God wrote in a private letter, "Love — the word — it brings noth-ing. — I am told God loves me — and yet the reality of darkness and coldness and emptiness is so great that nothing touches my soul."[95]

She was like Mary Magdalene at the tomb, in a sort of blind-ness, overcome with grief, who gasps between her tears, "They have taken away my Lord and I do not know where they have laid him" (John 20:13).

Now, granted, her darkness was exceptional for its depth and duration. No one can compare their interior sufferings with one who was chosen to bear such a cross as a part of her apostolate. In time, she would come to understand her long night as a special gift. But every Christian who has said yes to God will know that there is a dimmer switch in God's hands and that there is a reason why Mother Teresa would write: "If I ever become a saint — I will surely be one of 'darkness.' I will continually be absent from heaven — to light the light of those in darkness on earth."[96]

Why do we need a patron saint of darkness?

If we have intentionally set out on the Christian journey of faith, we will find out.

We will pass through beautiful and consoling hours of broad daylight, the muted dusk of aridity, and eventually experience the

[95] Ibid., 35.
[96] Ibid., 105.

soft, melancholic fade of twilight. We may hesitate then, unsure of ourselves and of God as the shadows lengthen and obscure our familiar footings. But if we keep going—and we must—we will pass a long purgation, and then the evening will inevitably blink into a deeper darkness.

And in the starless center of the spiritual journey the saints tell us to expect something called the "Dark Night."

After months of aridity, St. Elizabeth of the Trinity would find herself entering a crushing darkness, her soul peering into her own nothingness and encountering only (what felt like) a gaping hole where God should be.

And though she kept it hidden from all but her superiors (her letters to family and friends from the time mention only the cross but not her personal suffering), her interior crucifixion would reach such a state that even her vocation was obscured and all but un-recognizable. Shaken to her core, she once again surrendered her call to the silent voice she had once heard so clearly.

There were human components—as there often are. Summer had turned into a dark, damp winter, the monotony of the rule may have set in along with anxiety about approaching vows, and she struggled with the return of a stifling scrupulosity.

Still, in this case, something else was moving, something divine, a tender hand pruning a precious vine so that it could bear fruit in due season. Elizabeth remained supple and allowed God, unseen, to continue His deep and delicate work in her soul. She could not see or feel Jesus, but she may have heard in her soul a faint echo of His cry: "My God, my God, why has thou forasken me?" (Matt. 27:46).

At its darkest point, a soul in such a place may wonder as it gropes clumsily around for the face of the God it longs for: *Does God love me?*

And another terrifying thought: *Do I love God?*

"The impression does not belong to reality. God loves this soul, and the most beautiful proof of His love is that He is drawing it to Himself and binding its whole will. Consequently it is not at all true that this soul does not love the Lord. Quite the contrary! Its love for God is being developed in immense proportions," Fr. Gabriel of St. Mary Magdalen reassures us in *Union with God according to St. John of the Cross*.[97]

As awful as it is, though, the darkness of this spiritual state is not an evil but rather a grace. It is a time of visitation: although the Divine Visitor is silent, He is closer than ever. Perhaps it would be accurate to say that He is not the one hidden, but the soul, unknowing, is buried in such a deep embrace it can no longer see the familiar profile of Jesus. It is spending Holy Saturday in a tomb with a hidden Christ who is breaking thousands of years of bondage.

It is a grace that is given for the ultimate purpose of the human person: union with God, a grace that gets to the very root of our broken nature—every obstacle to union sweetly, painfully obliterated in this place of purification. The will is unbound and free to make a total gift of itself to God.

"The stains of the old self still linger in the spirit, although they may not be apparent or perceptible. If these are not wiped away by the use of soap and strong lye of this purgative night, the spirit will be unable to reach the purity of divine union," teaches St. John of the Cross.[98] His writings, along with those of Teresa of Avila, are foundational to the understanding of both the night and

---

[97] Fr. Gabriel of St. Mary Magdalen, *Union with God according to St. John of the Cross* (Manchester, NH: Sophia Institute Press, 2019), 147.

[98] St. John of the Cross, *The Dark Night*, in *The Collected Works of St. John of the Cross*, trans. Kieran Kavanaugh, O.C.D. (Washington: ICS Publications, 1991), 397.

the union it led to, and so the Church has long looked to these Carmelite Doctors as guides to the interior life. In this respect, St. Elizabeth was not only entering her own spiritual suffering but also experiencing fully the very particular charism of her order. No doubt her familiarity with these two spiritual giants and their writings would offer her a degree of comfort. Additionally, her superior, Mother Germaine, was well versed in the spiritual writings of these founders and thus was able to understand something of what her young novice was feeling, to take it in stride, and not see it as necessarily an obstacle to her vocation. (It might have been, in fact, a confirmation of it.)

Pope St. John Paul II wrote, "The saints offer us precious insights which enable us to understand more easily the intuition of faith, thanks to the special enlightenment which some of them have received from the Holy Spirit, or even through their personal experience of those terrible states of trial which the mystical tradition describes as the 'dark night.' Not infrequently the saints have undergone something akin to Jesus' experience on the Cross in the paradoxical blending of bliss and pain."[99]

But not everyone would understand.

The Dominican priest who had given Elizabeth direction even before she entered, Fr. Vallee, was unfamiliar with the Carmelite spiritual teachings and did not recognize the Dark Night as such. He saw her lack of joy and troubled spirit as signs that her community was being too harsh and exacting. Upset, he refused to see her anymore for direction. And she limped her way toward her final vows, suffering greatly.

Can you imagine the added degree of distress this apparent rejection would have caused? Spiritual directors—and really, all

---

[99] Pope John Paul II, Apostolic Letter *Novo Millennio Ineunte* (January 6, 2001), no. 27.

of us with any interest in the spiritual life — must have some degree of familiarity with the mystical reality of the Dark Night. In their inner loneliness, suffering souls can rarely see it for what it is, and a word of comfort and understanding can go a long way in soothing a raw spirit.

It is, admittedly, a difficult subject and as elusive as a butterfly at midnight. And in the end, we are reduced to wholly inadequate analogies that cannot begin to explain what is both painful and at the same time a gift beyond imagining. It is a paradox, but it is real, and all of us will walk in some degree of darkness in our lives. If we've given ourselves to Jesus, the darkness can be a sacred place, sanctified by the silence of God and by our surrender to Him of even our holiest desires.

St. Teresa of Calcutta, pray for us in our times of darkness.

To be in love and yet not to love, to live by faith and yet not to believe. To spend myself and yet to be in total darkness.[100]

—St. Teresa of Calcutta

---

[100] Murray, *I Loved Jesus in the Night*, 31.

A Divine Darkness

Questions for Reflection

What is the difference between a dark-night experience and spiritual aridity?

Why does God allow the soul to experience the feeling of abandonment in this spiritual place?

What is the soul actually experiencing?

How do the lives of the saints help us to understand our spiritual experiences?

23

A Living Smile

It was a Saturday in the spring of 2020, in the middle of the coronavirus pandemic, and I waited outside behind my strip of blue tape for my turn for confession. When I entered, the masked priest motioned me to a table across the room from him, so far away that I had to raise my voice to be heard. *I've never shouted a confession before*, I thought, as I took a seat. *But these are strange times we are in.*

"Bless me, Father, for I have sinned," I hollered. I cleared my throat and shifted in the chair. "I haven't been the easiest person to live with these last few months."

It was true. As the weeks had turned into months of quarantine and isolation and I resigned myself to my new role of homeschooling mom, as my college son had returned home and my husband began to work from the kitchen table, as all eight of us saw one day blur into another, into one long stretch and one (very) short fuse, well, let's just say I hadn't exactly risen to the occasion.

I had tried, I'll give myself that. I lowered my expectations and intentionally embraced my family's time together. I napped when I needed and snuck out for walks when I could. I tried to take care of myself so that I could take better care of the family. But too often I had ignored the unraveling edges of my spirit, rubbed raw in the unaccustomed stress. And sometimes I had made no attempt to hide my fatigue, irritation, and worry.

Sometimes we need to ask for help, and that's okay. But when we slam the pot lid or the door, or let a large sigh escape when we know others are listening ... well, sometimes we just want everyone to know just how much we are suffering. And that's not exactly what the saints would have done.

St. Thérèse of Lisieux wrote, "Often a single word, a friendly smile, is enough to give a depressed or lonely soul fresh life."[101] In the harsh conditions of the convent, how much life she must have radiated to the sisters, so often surprised by the "saint of the smile."

I can absolutely see her smile, too—photographs of the Little Flower always portray a tiny upturn at the corners of her mouth, a look laced with mischief and some wonderful secret. In contrast, St. Elizabeth of the Trinity always looked grave and thoughtful in her pictures, pondering deep things behind her eyes. Yet she, too, lived as a smile.

Sr. Elizabeth, as a young novice, was nearly overcome by her interior agony that first year after taking the habit. She confided her sufferings to her superiors, and that was good and necessary. But the other nuns had no idea of the turmoil going on in her heart. On the outside, Elizabeth was completely tranquil. She quietly went about her work, prayed deeply and devotedly, made herself utterly and openly and joyfully available, and never let it slip that she was suffering. Jesus knew. There was no need to burden others.

"Sister Anne-Marie ... would give a beautiful cameo portrait of Elizabeth in action: 'When one approached her, she was always smiling and always ready to do what was asked of her.' Yet even this praise falls short of giving the whole picture, for Elizabeth

---

[101] *The Story of a Soul*, 144.

went further—in two ways. Firstly, she did not just smile when accepting a task: she went so far as to give the impression that the person asking for help was doing her a favor!"[102]

"Try to put joy—not the joy you can feel but the joy of your will—into every irritation, every sacrifice," she wrote to her mother.[103] She knew that it was impossible to be happy all the time and not to be affected by the sinfulness or thoughtlessness of others. But it is a small but supreme act of charity to choose to smile despite hurt or disappointment in our hearts.

A smile communicates God to others and reflects back to them something of their own innate goodness.

Fr. Michael Gaitley, MIC, shares his discovery of the pamphlet the "Apostolate of Smiling" in his book, *"You Did It to Me": A Practical Guide to Mercy in Action.* It reads, in part:

> You are an apostle now, and your smile is your instrument for winning souls ...
> YOUR SMILE ...
> can bring new life and hope and courage into the hearts of the weary, the overburdened, the discouraged, the tempted, the despairing.
> YOUR SMILE ...
> can help to develop vocations if you are a priest, a brother, or a sister.
> YOUR SMILE ...
> can be the beginning of conversions to the faith.
> YOUR SMILE ...
> can prepare the way for a sinner's return to God ...
> SMILE, TOO, AT GOD ...

---

[102] Mosley, *Elizabeth of the Trinity*, vol. 1, 295–296.
[103] Letter 317, in Nash, *Complete Works*, vol. 2, 338.

This Present Paradise

Smile at God in loving acceptance of whatever he sends into your life, and you will merit to have the radiantly Smiling Face of Christ gaze on you with special love throughout eternity.[104]

And because Jesus also suffered, and her trial was united to His, Elizabeth could indeed smile (although maybe with a quiet tear or two) at Jesus.

A soul united to Jesus is a living smile
that radiates Him and gives Him![105]

— St. Elizabeth of the Trinity

Mother Teresa of Calcutta said, "Jesus can demand a great deal from us. It is precisely in those instances when He demands a great deal from us that we should give Him a beautiful smile."[106]

Maybe, if we are in the world, we suspect that it is much easier to smile at Jesus than at one another. But Mother Teresa tells this story: "Some time ago a big group of professors came to our house in Calcutta. Before leaving, they said to me, 'Tell us something that will help us, that will help us become holy.' And I said to them, 'Smile at each other.' ... And one of them asked me, 'Are you married, Mother Teresa?' I said, 'Yes, and I sometimes find it very difficult to smile at my spouse, Jesus, because He can be very demanding.'"[107]

---

[104] Michael E. Gaitley, MIC, *"You Did it to Me"*: *A Practical Guide to Mercy in Action* (Stockbridge, MA: Marian Press, 2019), 42–44.

[105] Letter 252, in Nash, *Complete Works*, vol. 2, 236.

[106] Mother Teresa of Calcutta, *Love: A Fruit Always in Season*, ed. Dorothy S. Hunt (San Francisco: Ignatius Press, 1987), 185.

[107] Ibid., 186.

A Living Smile

She made it clear that part of her missionary work was simply to smile. And smile she did—at everyone.

"Let us always meet each other with a smile ... for a smile is the beginning of love," Mother Teresa said. "We shall never know all the good that a simple smile can do. We speak of our God, good, clement, and understanding; but are we the living proof of it? Those who suffer, can they see this goodness, this forgiving God, this real understanding in us? Never let anyone come to you without coming away better and happier. Everyone should see goodness in your face, in your eyes, in your smile."[108]

Smile at God, from whom every gift comes to us;
smile at the Father with ever more perfect prayer;
smile at the Holy Spirit;
smile at Jesus whom you approach at Mass, in Holy
Communion, and in Eucharistic adoration;
smile at the person who represents
Christ on earth: the Pope;
smile at your confessor, the one who personifies God
even when he challenges you to reject sin;
smile at the Blessed Virgin, to whose example you
must conform your life, so that, seeing you,
people might be led to holy thoughts;
smile at your Guardian Angel, because this angel has
been given to you by God to lead you into Paradise;
smile at your parents, brothers, and sisters,
even when they challenge your pride;
smile always in forgiving offenses;
smile in associating with others,

[108] Ibid., 184.

banishing all criticism and murmuring.
Smile at everyone the Lord sends you during the day.[109]

— St. Gianna Molla (known as "the Smile of God")

Questions for Reflection

Do you find it hard to smile or show joy
when you are tired, worried, or upset?

What does a simple expression — such as a
smile — do to lift your spirits when you are down?

How do your expressions reflect God to others?

---

[109] Giuliana Pelucchi, *Blessed Gianna Beretta Molla: A Woman's Life* (Boston: Pauline Books and Media, 2002), 61.

24

To Be a Bride

In the midst of her dark night, St. Elizabeth received some welcome news: her younger sister Guite was engaged to be married. Elizabeth noticed how "radiant" her sister was. "Her heart," she observed, "has been taken."[110] Her fiancé was Georges Chevignard, a banker and a cellist who fell in love not only with Guite but also with her musical talent—and enjoyed her accompaniment on the piano. (Together, they would create quite a score: nine children, including four nuns and a priest!) Mindful of Elizabeth, who would be unable to attend their wedding, they chose for the date October 15—the feast of St. Teresa of Avila.

Elizabeth promised her sister: "We will have the Blessed Sacrament exposed in the chapel that day, and while the Church consecrates your union, the Carmelite, the happy one chained by Christ, will spend the day at His feet becoming wholly praying, wholly adoring, for those 'two' whom God wishes to be 'one'!"[111]

The approaching marriage naturally made Elizabeth think of her state in life, her vocation as a religious sister who would never be a wife and mother in the worldly sense. Did "the happy one chained

---

[110] Letter 130, in Nash, *Complete Works*, vol. 2, 59.
[111] Letter 135, in Nash, *Complete Works*, vol. 2, 64.

by Christ" perhaps feel a certain touch of wonder or longing for what might have been in her life?

And yet she knew that by forsaking those goods, she was giving a radical yes to Christ, her Divine Bridegroom, setting aside "a whole life to be spent in silence and adoration, a heart-to-heart with the Spouse!"[112]

She knew that every woman was created to be a bride, and she lived that. She wrote a meditation on this "divine reality" the summer before Guite's wedding, reflecting on what it means to be a bride of Christ and to enter into a cooperative, generative union with Him: "[To be a bride] is to be fruitful, a co-redemptrix, to engender souls to grace, to multiply those adopted by the Father, those redeemed by Christ, to be co-heirs of His glory." She says, "it is a marriage, a fixed state, because it is the indissoluble union of wills and hearts."[113]

Later, after she had professed her vows, she would reflect: "I heard the Church say 'Veni sponsa Christi' (Come, bride of Christ); she consecrated me, and now all is 'consummated'. Rather, everything is beginning, for profession is only a dawn; and each day my 'life as a bride' seems to me more beautiful, more luminous, more enveloped in peace and love."[114]

"One cannot correctly understand virginity — a woman's consecration in virginity — without referring to spousal love," writes Pope St. John Paul II.

The natural spousal predisposition of the feminine personality finds a response in virginity understood this way.

---

[112] Letter 149, in Nash, *Complete Works*, vol. 2, 81.
[113] Mosley, *Elizabeth of the Trinity*, vol. 1, 234–235.
[114] Letter 169, in Nash, *Complete Works*, vol. 2, 110.

To Be a Bride

Women, called from the "beginning" to be loved and to love, in a vocation to virginity find Christ first of all as the Redeemer who 'loved until the end' through his total gift of self; and they respond to this gift with a "sincere gift" of their whole lives. They thus give themselves to the divine Spouse, and this personal gift tends to union, which is properly spiritual in character. Through the Holy Spirit's action a woman becomes "one spirit" with Christ the Spouse.[115]

The Church understands a life of consecrated virginity not in sterile terms but as a sincere, total, and fruitful gift of the self that is spousal in nature. It is Jesus who takes the consecrated virgin for Himself, and she becomes a sign of the Church as Bride and a foreshadowing of the eternal wedding feast.

This is a breathtaking reality that the world simply cannot see. The consecrated woman stands as a sign of contradiction: what she seems to have given up, she has actually gained in a far more real way than the rest of us can know this side of eternity.

The woman who embraces the religious life knows this secret. We catch a glimpse of it in *The Story of a Soul*, when St. Thérèse of Lisieux recounts a visit to the convent by her newly married cousin Jeanne Guérin. This was shortly after Thérèse had pronounced her vows as a Carmelite and had herself become a bride — a bride of Christ.

Struck by Jeanne's wedding invitations, she wrote her one of her own:

[115] Pope John Paul II, Apostolic Letter *Mulieris Dignitatem* (August 15, 1988), 20.

ALMIGHTY GOD
The Creator of Heaven & Earth
and Ruler of the World
and
THE MOST GLORIOUS VIRGIN MARY
Queen of the Court of Heaven
Invite you to the Spiritual Marriage of their August Son
JESUS, KING OF KINGS,
and LORD OF LORDS
with
Little Thérèse Martin,
now a Lady and Princess of
the Kingdoms of the Childhood
and Passion of Jesus, given in dowry
by her Divine Spouse,
from whom she holds the titles of nobility:
OF THE CHILD JESUS and OF THE HOLY FACE.
It was not possible to invite you to the Wedding Feast
celebrated on Mount Carmel on September 8, 1890,
only the Celestial Choir being admitted.
You are nevertheless invited to the Bride's RECEPTION
tomorrow, the Day of Eternity, when Jesus,
the Son of God, will come in splendor
on the clouds of Heaven to judge
the Living and the Dead.
The hour being uncertain,
please hold yourself in readiness and watch.[116]

---

[116] *The Story of a Soul*, 100–101.

To Be a Bride

A consecrated woman is then, in her very being, prophetic. She points to a reality far beyond herself, one that we are all invited to see fulfilled in our own spiritual lives in heaven. She stands as a beautiful living icon of what we await at the end of time—a bridal mystery. She calls us by the example of her life to keep our lamps lit. And for that we should be forever grateful.

Thank you, consecrated women! Following the example of the greatest of women, the Mother of Jesus Christ, the Incarnate Word, you open yourselves with obedience and fidelity to the gift of God's love. You help the Church and all mankind to experience a "spousal" relationship to God, one which magnificently expresses the fellowship which God wishes to establish with his creatures.

—Pope St. John Paul II, *Letter to Women*

Questions for Reflection

What does a consecrated religious gain by giving up marriage and family?

How does a religious brother or sister stand as a sign of contradiction?

What do they image for you?

25

The Power of Intercessory Prayer

It happens almost every Monday morning: dozens of women of all ages and stages meet in our parish courtyard, corralling sticky kids and cradling cups of steaming coffee as we gather for a weekly study group.

We love learning about the Faith together and diving into the lives of particular saints or Church documents. We relish getting into deep discussions about situations in our lives or events in the world and how—inevitably—the Church has the answers before we have the questions.

The format of the group has developed over the years, and something has emerged that I hadn't originally scheduled in or expected. We had always opened with prayer, but slowly, without my realizing it at first, a time of intercessory prayer began to grow into its own thing. We started to begin our meetings with a time of long, intense petition not only for ourselves but also for our family members, friends, and suffering people we had never met but who began to come out of nowhere and ask us to pray for them: "I hear you have a powerful group of intercessors. Will you ask them to pray for me?" We found ourselves being sought out, and finally I had to ask my friend Michelle, who has a charism for it, to take over all of these petitions and compile them—or we'd never have been able to keep track, much less keep up.

So every week we lay them before the Lord and pray over them together, begging for healing, for answers, for relief—for God's will, and for our own embrace of it. It is becoming clear to me that rather than a distraction or delay of our study, it may be a charism of our group and is most likely part of the Lord's original intent in its design.

This makes sense, because it is part of *our design*. We are called to pray for each other: "Since Abraham, intercession—asking on behalf of another—has been characteristic of a heart attuned to God's mercy. In the age of the Church, Christian intercession participates in Christ's, as an expression of the communion of saints. In intercession, he who prays looks 'not only to his own interests, but also the interests of others,' even to the point of praying for those who do him harm' (Phil. 2:4; cf. Acts 7:60; Luke 23:28, 34)" (CCC 2635).

In other words, it is Jesus who prays for all us before the Father. But then we enter into His very prayer and extend it in a way with our own. "I appeal to you, brethren," St. Paul says, "by our Lord Jesus Christ and by the love of the Spirit, to strive together with me in your prayers to God on my behalf" (Rom. 15:30).

Our prayer acknowledges before God who we are and our need for Him: "We are creatures who are not our own beginning, not the masters of our adversity, not our own last end. We are sinners who as Christians know that we have turned away from the Father. Our petition is already a turning back to Him." And so we "ask, beseech, plead, invoke, entreat, cry out" for each other and all of our needs (CCC 2629). We pray that God will put things in right order in our lives; we pray for health, for safety, for discernment, for our welfare and well-being. We pray that God will make all things new, especially that He will restore fully our relationship with Him and align our will totally with His, so that everything that happens will be a means to drawing us nearer to Him, for His glory and our eternal happiness.

And to pray this way for the other? Well, the beautiful irony is that it is we who are blessed. It is a graced moment from God to be asked to pray for another, a sign of His love that He wants us to participate in His immense work of redemption, to make some part of His plan dependent on our prayers. Let me say that again: *to make some part of His plan dependent on our prayers*.

"God bestows many things on us out of His liberality, even without our asking for them: but that He wishes to bestow certain things on us at our asking, is for the sake of our good, namely, that we may acquire confidence in having recourse to God, and that we may recognize in Him the Author of our goods,"[117] writes St. Thomas Aquinas in the *Summa Theologica*. That's a mouthful, but put in other words, from all eternity, the Lord has many blessings for us, and most are given freely, but some are reserved until we ask for them. So it is not that we change God's mind, but that He has determined that some things will be set in motion only by our prayers. Why? Because He wants to have a relationship with us, a dynamic exchange of friendship, confidence, intimacy, and love.

It's amazing. We have Jesus Christ as our Mediator, the Holy Spirit as our Advocate, Mary as our interceding Mother, our guardian angels as our constant, attentive intercessors, and the saints: "when they entered the joy of their Master, they were 'put in charge of many things' (cf. Matt. 25:21). Their intercession is their most exalted service to God's plan. We can and should ask them to intercede for us and the whole world" (CCC 2683).

We also have one another. Personally and communally called to pray, we are part of this glorious communion.

---

[117] St. Thomas Aquinas, *Summa Theologica* II-II, q. 83, art. 2.

This Present Paradise

Some religious orders, including the Carmelites, have a charism for intercessory prayer. Elizabeth of the Trinity reflects that particular availability to the needs of others in her letters, always ready to lay their intentions before the Lord in her constant prayer. "Indeed, she understood precisely that her grace of election placed her as a woman of prayer and a mediator in the heart of the Church, as a means and instrument of God's love for all brothers and sisters."[118]

As a religious, Elizabeth would often be asked to pray for the sick and the suffering, and she gladly helped them to shoulder their burdens, seeing it as part of her call. She wanted them to leave it to her and to her community, who always joined their prayers together for the many petitions from the suffering, anxious souls in the world.

In one letter, Elizabeth writes to her friend's mother in response to her request for prayers for a mutual friend's husband, who has become very sick. "I recommend your intentions to [God]. Do not doubt Him, dear Madame, abandon everything to Him, as well as your little friend ... for her mission is to pray unceasingly, and you know how much that holds true for you! ... I kiss my dear Françoise whom I love so much and your sweet Marie-Louise. I pray fervently for them, and I am always all yours; don't you feel that?"[119]

I'm sure she did feel it. That's part of the power of our prayer, too, to help others, in some mysterious way, to carry their crosses and to trust God in their most cruciform moments. How often have we heard someone say, "It was your prayers that got me through"? That's not just a sentiment: it is a real spiritual exchange that people experience whenever someone carries another in his or her prayers. It is being part of the Body of Christ, being bound to one

---

[118] Balthasar, *Two Sisters in the Spirit*, 413.
[119] Letter 157, in Nash, *Complete Works*, vol. 2, 94.

another. Elizabeth asked her mother, "Don't you feel my prayer that is constantly rising up to Him and descending to you?"[120]

So, when we are in line at the store or making dinner or bringing in the mail and something within us whispers a particular name, unexpectedly calling someone to mind, let's not dismiss that heavenly invitation. Let's say a prayer. That someone might need our prayers more than we know, and if we dismiss it in our busyness, we just might miss out on a grace that will never come in the same way again.

And next time we say, "I'll pray for you," let's remember the potential power of those words. They have the capacity to change things, and not least of all our own hearts.

Whoever enters Carmel is not lost to his own (loved ones) but is theirs fully for the first time; it is our vocation to stand before God for all.[121]

—St. Teresa Benedicta of the Cross (Edith Stein)

Questions for Reflection

Have you experienced the power of intercessory prayer—either as the petitioner or the recipient?

Which saints do you count on as your team of intercessors?

Will you add St. Elizabeth to your team?

---

[120] Letter 176, in Nash, *Complete Works*, vol. 2, 122.
[121] St. Teresa Benedicta of the Cross to Fritz Kaufmann, in *The Collected Works of Edith Stein*, vol. 5, *Self-Portrait in Letters*, ed. Dr. L. Gelber (Washington DC: ICS Publications, 1993), 177.

26

Saints Are People Too

My heart plummeted. As I had emptied the car of groceries that steamy summer day, there was one thing that I could not carry in because it was not where it should have been. My purse was nowhere in sight.

The shopping cart.

I must have left it in the cart when I loaded the bags, I thought miserably. I flew back to store, berating myself the entire way, spilling tears over the steering wheel. *It's just like me—I am so forgetful! I lose everything!*

I pulled into the parking lot, noticing immediately that there were no carts left where I had been parked. NO! I dashed into the store. As soon as I reached the service desk, I choked out my story, and the clerk reached under the counter and pulled out my purse. Someone had brought it in, totally intact.

I dissolved in tears again, this time in gratitude for an unnamed stranger, kind and honest, and a sign of God's protection that day.

Another time, I "lost" my cell phone at a work conference. I ran around the convention center, begging security guards to let me into the closed auditorium to scour the aisles. After a long back-and-forth over walkie-talkies, they reluctantly agreed to escort me into the vast darkness, shining flashlights under rows of seats until I had to admit defeat. I dejectedly returned to my hotel room—and found the phone in my bag.

My husband is used to my doubling back home to grab a forgotten list or phone or being late for an appointment because I misplaced my keys. I never buy nice sunglasses because I have to replace them so often. I can't, for the life of me, remember birthdays or phone numbers. I have to heat up my coffee five times a day because I set it down on a bookshelf or the washing machine and promptly forget about it. It's frustrating! But—it's me.

It was also St. Elizabeth of the Trinity.

When she was a young girl, she wrote in an essay that she was, "cheerful and, I must admit, a bit scatterbrained."[122] In the convent, she was given the job of second (assistant) portress: she was in charge of communicating with the extern sisters, Carmelites in her order who had access to the outside world. When these sisters needed something from the enclosed convent, they would find Elizabeth ready at the "turn" to help secure an item or deliver a message. She was ready, she was willing—but she was also forgetful. Her superiors were exasperated. "Elizabeth was often so recollected that this made her forgetful in material things. This led her to cause great inconvenience, for she was always losing the keys—of the turn, the enclosure, and even the enclosure door! She would conscientiously take down a message—only to forget the name of the sister to whom she was supposed to give it!"[123]

I suppose she was daydreaming about Jesus. A little too much Mary when it was time to be Martha, maybe? (I wonder if she had a devotion to St. Anthony, invoked by countless Catholics when things go missing.) But her absentmindedness reminds us that Elizabeth was human. We need that reminder sometimes. We need

---

[122] Mosley, *Elizabeth of the Trinity*, vol. 1, 38.
[123] Ibid., 272.

heroic virtue; we need inspiring stories. Every now and then, we love to hear about a heavenly vision, an astonishing miracle, a bit of levitating. But once in a while, when our own humanity hits us over the head, we find comfort in knowing that saints are people too. And knowing this can help us to not admit defeat.

I asked my friends, "Which saints can you identify with?" Their replies are telling: Pope St. John Paul II, who was often late (distracted by the Eucharist, apparently!); St. Thérèse, who fell asleep at prayer; her mother, St. Zélie Martin, who stressed about being a working mom; St. Thomas Aquinas, who was afraid of thunderstorms; Fr. Solanus Casey, who had a squeaky voice and little talent for the violin he insisted on playing (to the dismay of his fellow friars). We can identify with clumsy saints, impulsive saints, doubtful saints, saints who wouldn't be saints until they mastered their addictions and surrendered their fragmented lives to God—saints who say to us: I am one of you.

And so, suffice it to say, St. Elizabeth endeared herself to me in her forgetfulness. This doesn't excuse my faults as much as it suggests that there's hope for me, for all of us imperfect humans.

At the same time she was losing the keys, she had "found," gloriously, something that she had lost for over a year: the consolation of God.

January 11, 1903—Epiphany Sunday—she had professed her final vows of chastity, poverty, and obedience to her superiors and the rule of the Carmelites. Right up until that day, and even as she made her vows and lay prostrate before the altar, she was still very much in a state of darkness.

Immediately afterward, however, the night suddenly lightened into a long-awaited dawn, breaking radiantly across her spirit like a sudden sunrise spilling open the day.

She would not experience the same flood of consolations she had before, but there was peace in her soul, a soul matured by immense interior suffering. She was now tasting a more subtle sweetness—the sweetness of a deep, quiet faith. And that was one thing that would never be lost in her life again.

Questions for Reflection

Which saints do you identify with most?

Have you ever had trouble seeing saints as human and relatable?

Can you relate to St. Elizabeth of the Trinity in any way?

27

My Every Act Is Love

A single action — even the least and most insignificant —
done with the view of pleasing God alone, and of
glorifying Him, is worth infinitely more, so to speak,
than many actions in themselves of the greatest value
and worth that spring from other motives.[124]

Five years ago, a friend who works for a radio station invited me to an annual luncheon, with an address by our bishop, put on by a prominent Catholic foundation. Since I like my friend, and I like my bishop, and I happen to like lunch, I agreed to go. I lined up a sitter, pulled my favorite navy blazer out of the back of the closet, and drove downtown.

As we made our way to a round table in the back of the room, I noticed many well-known faces. As the choir finished singing and we were served salads on tiny glass plates, the women at our table began to introduce themselves. All of a sudden, I realized something that, in my naivete, I had missed until now. *This is a lunch for leaders.*

[124] Lorenzo Scupoli, *Spiritual Combat* (Manchester, NH: Sophia Institute Press, 2002), 36.

This Present Paradise

Every one of the lovely women had a position of prominence or influence, and as they began exchanging business cards, I fiddled with my napkin. Then the inevitable moment: the board member of Catholic Charities turned to me. "And what do you do?" she asked with a kind smile. "I work part-time at my parish," I said, feeling the color rise to my cheeks. A few blank stares and nice nods, and they put their cards away. The chicken suddenly tasted like cardboard. "She's amazing at it!" chirped my friend, trying to save me. But it was too late. I felt very small—so very small.

The rest of the lunch was nice, the conversation pleasant, the bishop wonderful. Gradually my flushed cheeks faded, and I got over myself. But as I slid into the car afterward, I sat for a moment to reflect and became emotional again. I was really surprised at the depth of my own shame in that conversation at lunch. I had never wanted to be anyone other than a wife and mom. I had no ambitions to be a leader or have a position of influence. I had just wanted to have lunch. And yet there I was, wanting to hide because I was "nobody."

By God's great grace, I allowed it to be an opportunity. I decided then and there, sitting in my Suburban, to be the best "nobody" I could be. I remembered how St. Thérèse said that to pick up a pin for love could save a soul. Well, I could do that. I pick up a lot of stuff every day, I figured. And that's good: I have a lot of souls entrusted to me. I embraced nothingness in that moment. I decided to go home and redouble my efforts at loving God in the small things. That was all I had, and it was all I could do. I didn't sit on a board or manage a radio station or run a hospital. I folded socks and wrote a little bit and kissed bumped foreheads and stocked up on ground beef when it was on sale. But I did—or tried to do—all of it because I love God and the little people He hid within. I pulled out of the parking garage and merged onto the freeway, thinking, *that beats a board any day.*

My Every Act Is Love

Elizabeth of the Trinity, as one of the first followers of St. Thérèse, also tried to do absolutely everything in a spirit of self-forgetfulness and love. Remember, she had started this habit as a young girl, and it had transformed her stubborn temperament. This theme of humility and embracing the little things in life is so important that it is worth revisiting in her adult years.

In the convent, she was not only the second (assistant) "turn sister" but was also, as a talented seamstress, an overqualified but humble and obedient second habit sister. "Did I tell you," she wrote to her aunts, "that I was the habit sister, which means I am responsible for mending the habits of the community under the direction of the sister in charge of that office, she furnishes me with work and explains it to me, and I do it in the solitude of our dear cell. You would be edified if you saw the poverty of our clothes. After twenty or thirty years, you can guess they have a few patches.... I love to sew this dear serge, which I so desired to wear and in which it is so good to live in Carmel."[125] While she worked at her lowly task, she prayed, grateful to have busy hands but a heart free to bury itself in the love of Christ. St. Thérèse picked up a pin, and Elizabeth delicately plied a needle. But, again, the motive was the same: tiny actions, great love.

These two young Carmelites have a complementary mission to the laity today: You, too, they seem to say, have a life filled with opportunities to turn nothings into treasures. Look beyond the apparent smallness of the stuff of your life. See beneath it. It is weighted with eternity. It is infused with grace. It is waiting only for your yes for its real power to be unleashed. And you will feel the tremendous force of love when the dam breaks in your soul and you are carried by the current of your hidden acts straight into the Heart of Jesus — when "all the rivers of the soul, which are so

---

[125] Letter 258, in Nash, *Complete Works*, vol. 2, 242.

immense they already resemble seas, go to lose themselves in the Ocean of divine love."[126]

One day, while Sister Elizabeth of the Trinity was hurrying to complete a task in the convent, one of the older sisters stopped her to ask what she was doing. "Oh, my mother," she answered, "I am loving."[127]

I am loving.

Whatever that errand was—probably some insignificant task—it didn't matter. It had been made invaluable. It had been turned into an act of pure love.

Everything is made infinite when it is infused with love for God.

Suddenly, what is before us we see as His will and an opportunity to love Him. Let's pray for that purity of intention with each little thing we do.

My every act is love.[128]

—St. John of the Cross

Questions for Reflection

Have you ever felt small and insignificant?

How can we turn small acts into great opportunities?

What small things can you offer to God today?

---

[126] Letter 293, in Nash, *Complete Works*, vol. 2, 297.
[127] Mosley, *Elizabeth of the Trinity*, vol. 1, 290.
[128] St. John of the Cross, *Spiritual Canticle*, in *Collected Works*, 475.

28

Called to Carmel for the Persecution

My very dear Mama,
  Our Reverend Mother must have told you that because of recent events we are taking a few precautionary measures in case we should have to leave our dear cloister. I'd be very grateful if you'd give me your skirt pattern right away.[129]

Elizabeth had chosen to enter religious life at a tumultuous time for the Catholic Church in France. The nuns may have been set apart from the world, but they were not unaware that tensions were high between the Church and the aggressively anti-Catholic French government. Determined to wipe out the Church's influence on society, the secular government at the time outlawed Catholic education in the name of "freedom," forcing the closure of thousands of Catholic schools. Tens of thousands of religious who had given their lives to teaching and sharing the Faith had no choice but to leave.

Church property everywhere was being confiscated. In all, thirty-eight Carmelite congregations had to leave France, including the first French Carmel established there. In this time of uncertainty, the

---

[129] Letter 148, in Nash, *Complete Works*, vol. 2, 80.

Dijon community prepared for the worst. They prudently secured a farmhouse in Belgium, stored some their most precious furniture and statues, and made street clothes so that they could slip away at a moment's notice, ready, if necessary, to disappear from their homeland in their own little diaspora.

It never did come to that. But the Carmelites in Dijon were forced to close their chapel to the public by government order, and the nuns lived in a period of great uncertainty: How long would they be allowed to remain?

The convent was prepared but trusting and tranquil. Elizabeth was not apathetic or indifferent—but she was calm and accepted the fact that she could once again be asked to live as "a Carmelite in the world" if the walls of their beloved convent were breached by the persecutors of the Church. In fact, the idea of suffering for the sake of Christ brought her consolation, which she shared with her aunts:

> Thank [God] for having called your little Elizabeth to Carmel for the persecution; I do not know what awaits us, and this perspective of having to suffer because I am His delights my soul. I love my dear cloister so much, and sometimes I have wondered if I don't love this dear little cell too much, where it is good to be "alone with the Alone." Perhaps one day He will ask me to sacrifice it. I am ready to follow Him everywhere, and my soul will say with St. Paul: "Who will separate me from the love of Christ?" I have within me a solitude where He dwells, and nothing can take that away from me![130]

We may not anticipate becoming refugees, forced to leave our homes in order to practice our Faith. We may very well find, however,

---

[130] Letter 162, in Nash, *Complete Works*, vol. 2, 101.

that practicing our Faith—which we do everywhere—will become harder and harder. We Catholics do not worship only on Sundays during Mass: we worship with our very lives. We worship in the workplace, in the classroom, at the doctor's office—and it may be in those very places that we find ourselves defending our religious freedom more and more. We may find a swirl of persecution every time we open our front doors or turn on our televisions or engage in conversation. We may find our words hijacked: "gender," "love," "choice," "privacy," "marriage." We may find our churches burned, our statues defaced, our objections silenced. We may be told to be tolerant of wrongs—or even to cooperate with them—because others think them right. But we know we can't separate prayer from actions. To expect us to do so and to penalize us and censure us when we do not is a violation of our religious freedom. Even more fundamentally, it is a violation of our dignity as persons and our right to seek and live the truth. Such coercion is an infringement of both divine and natural law.

"For the first time in Western Christian civilization, the kingdom of anti-God has acquired political form and social substance and stands over and against Christianity as a counter-Church with its own dogmas, its own scriptures, its own infallibility, its own hierarchy, its own missionaries, and its own invisible head—too terrible to be named,"[131] Archbishop Fulton Sheen warned us decades ago. "Yes," Elizabeth predicted, even long before that: "The future is very dark."[132]

But still, there's so much hope. The Lord loves to breathe new life into His Church even when forces outside seek to tear down and confiscate and plant twisted stakes in what is sacred: our homes,

[131] Fulton J. Sheen, *Characters of the Passion* (Kettering, Ohio: Angelico Press, 2015), 28.
[132] Letter 160, in Nash, *Complete Works*, vol. 2, 99.

our churches, our schools, our laws, our courtrooms. There's a secret weapon He never fails to bring out: He brings forth holiness. He makes martyrs. He grows saints in hidden places.

At the turn of the century, it looked as if the earthly forces were winning a decisive victory in France and Catholicism was being humiliated and beaten back. A little nun in Dijon, however, was saying yes to God. In her every prayer, her every smile and tender letter, every movement of surrender and accepted suffering and every act of worship, St. Elizabeth was battling and defeating a great darkness. Through her (and other small, hidden saints of the time), God was invisibly but surely renewing His Church—and the world—through the graces of their lives and the legacy of their simple but powerful teaching. What the world sought to stamp out, God, in His great and unrelenting love, *raised right back up*.

We can be the hidden saints of our time. We are called to nothing less. Earthly kingdoms may rise or crumble around us, but what really matters is that, as Elizabeth pointed out, the one real Kingdom has been established in our souls. Our interior lives, like hidden wells, spill out over the spiritual landscape of our countries and transform the world. We may never know the effects that our prayers and sacrifices have. But we can be sure they are joining with Christ to work all things for good (see Rom. 8:28). We may feel powerless against faltering freedoms or a culture war that seems all but lost, but besides being promised the ultimate victory, we've been well equipped for every battle and skirmish. We drive back darkness with every act of charity or humility and every Hail Mary and every moment we forget ourselves for the sake of another. We will win by laying down our lives one day at a time.

That's why Archbishop Sheen can give this message of hope: "But whatever be the reason for these trying days, of this we may be certain: the Christ Who suffered under Pontius Pilate signed Pilate's death warrant; it was not Pilate who signed Christ's. Christ's

Called to Carmel for the Persecution

Church will be attacked, scorned, and ridiculed, but it will never be destroyed. The enemies of God will never be able to dethrone the heavens of God, nor to empty the tabernacles of their Eucharistic Lord, nor to cut off all absolving hands, but they may devastate the earth."[133]

In the end, my Immaculate Heart will Triumph.

—Our Lady of Fatima, July 13, 1917

Questions for Reflection

Where do we find our freedoms threatened right now?

How can you stand for truth and life in
a culture of deception and death?

Where do you see the greatest signs of hope?

[133] Sheen, *Characters of the Passion*, 31.

29

To Be an Apostle with You

Several years ago, I was awakened suddenly in the middle of the night and prompted to pray for a priest. I had known him for only one year; he was the principal of my grade school when I was eight years old. I said a Hail Mary, rolled over, and tried to go back to sleep. But something inside moved me to find out what had happened to this kind man who had personally prepared me for my first confession.

Urged by an interior summons and unable to sleep until I obeyed, I obligingly slipped out of bed and tiptoed to the computer.

With my hands poised over the keyboard, I realized that I didn't remember his last name. Honestly, I didn't think I had ever known it. *What am I even doing?* I wondered. Then, with a flash of clarity, as if someone were dictating to me, I suddenly knew what it was.

When I typed it in, his obituary flashed onto the screen. He had died two days before. And the obituary had been posted just moments ago—right when I had been awakened.

There's more to that story. But the first and most important message to me in that instant was the absolute and fundamental importance of praying for our priests.

This Present Paradise

It's something that the cloistered Carmelites have known well and taken to heart. From behind the walls of the convents, the sisters have seen it as part of their vocation to offer their prayers and sacrifices in a particular way for those commissioned to be "other Christs" and to spread the gospel throughout the world. This is the reason St. Thérèse, who never left her convent after she entered at fifteen, could be named patroness of the missions by Pope Pius XI in 1927, just two years after she was canonized.

Like her spiritual sister, Elizabeth of the Trinity had a great love for the priesthood. She was particularly devoted to Canon Angles, the priest to whom she had first entrusted the secret of her vocation. She would write to him as a spiritual daughter throughout her years in the convent, always remembering him in her prayers and valuing the power of his priestly prayers for her, particularly the "perfect prayer," the Mass: "I know," she wrote to him, "that you are praying for me every day at Holy Mass. Oh, won't you please place me in the chalice so my soul may be wholly bathed in this blood of my Christ for which I so thirst!"[134] In return, she assured him a "large share" of her own prayers.[135]

This beautiful reciprocity and complementarity of prayer took on another rich dimension when Elizabeth was asked to "adopt" a missionary to China, Henri Beaubis, to pray for and to encourage. Her inspired letters to him—some of her best—reveal that she had a rich understanding of the mysteriously apostolic side of her own vocation. She wrote to him:

> I am praying fervently for you, that God may invade all the powers of your soul, that He may make you live in communion with His whole Mystery, that everything in you

---

[134] Letter 131, in Nash, *Complete Works*, vol. 2, 60.
[135] Letter 190, in Nash, *Complete Works*, vol. 2, 142.

be divine and marked with His seal, so that you may be another Christ working for the glory of the Father! You are praying for me, too, aren't you? I want to be an apostle with you, from the depths of my dear solitude in Carmel, I want to work for the glory of God.... May our souls be one in Him, and while you bring Him to souls, I will remain, like Mary Magdalene, silent and adoring, close to the Master, asking him to make your word fruitful in souls. "Apostle, Carmelite," it is all one![136]

It was her desire that through his work and her prayer, they would draw down graces upon the world.

There was also to be a priest in the family: Elizabeth was introduced to her sister's brother-in-law, the seminarian André Chevignard. Because he was nearby in the diocesan seminary, he was able to visit her in the convent parlor and speak to her from behind the closed grille. Elizabeth added him to her prayers, and he received the benefit of an entire convent's friendship: the community "adopted" him and was delighted when he chose to celebrate his first Mass in their chapel.

Elizabeth was sensitive to a particularly difficult struggle in this seminarian's life. She desired to bring him peace in what was a turbulent time not only for the Church in France but for their diocese in particular. The bishop of Dijon seemed to be siding more with the anti-Catholic government than with Rome, and for that he would eventually be asked to resign. We can imagine what anxiety this would cause a young man in the local seminary. Elizabeth assured him, "My soul loves to unite with yours in one single prayer for the Church, for the diocese."[137] "I have prayed

---

[136] Letter 124, in Nash, *Complete Works*, vol. 2, 53.
[137] Letter 191, in Nash, *Complete Works*, vol. 2, 144.

for you and continue to do so every day," she said, "and I remain profoundly united to you in Him who is an immensity of love and who fills us overflowing on all sides."[138]

St. Thérèse also exercised her spiritual maternity in this exquisite way, promising union in God to the seminarian she considered her spiritual brother, Maurice Bellière: "United in Him, our souls will be able to save many others, for this kindly Jesus has said: 'If two among you agree together on something which they ask from my Father, it will be given to them.' Ah! What we ask of Him is to work for His glory, to love Him, and make Him loved. How should our union and prayers not be blessed?"

"I don't know the future," Thérèse wrote, "but if Jesus makes my premonition come true, I promise to remain your little sister in heaven. Far from being broken, our union will become a closer one, for then there will be no more cloister and no more grilles, and my soul will be free to fly with you to the missions far away. Our roles will still be the same. Yours will be apostolic labor, and mine will be prayer and love."[139]

Both Thérèse and Elizabeth saw clearly their apostolate of prayer and sacrifice for the Church's mission in the world: to give their lives, in layer upon layer of a daily sort of death, for the world's salvation, and do it all in complete hiddenness. To be able to cooperate specifically with someone in this task who was consecrated to be "another Christ" in the ministerial priesthood was an incredible joy.

"I love this thought," reflected Elizabeth, "that the life of the priest (and of the Carmelite) is an Advent that prepares for the Incarnation in souls."[140]

---

[138] Letter 199, in Nash, *Complete Works*, vol. 2, 157.
[139] Thérèse of Lisieux to Maurice Bellière, Lisieux, February 24, 1897, in *Maurice and Thérèse: The Story of a Love* by Patrick Ahern (New York: Doubleday, 1998), 82–85.
[140] Letter 250, in Nash, *Complete Works*, vol. 2, 232.

To Be an Apostle with You

Just as the young Carmelites were asked by their mother superiors to embrace the mission of prayer for priests in a particular way, the Church as our Mother invites all of us to participate in this all-important assignment. We all have a share in the universal priesthood of Christians through Baptism. More than that, we have a vocation to pray and sacrifice for the Church's ordained sons, a vocation which is now, praise God, spreading more and more out from the convents to the wider community. The need is too great not to summon the entire body of believers to their knees.

Have priests and seminarians ever needed our prayers more? Have these men in the front lines ever needed spiritual backup as they do now? Have they ever faced such cultural hostility, pressures from within and without the Church, incessant temptation from the enemy of souls who seeks to distort the image of Christ in the priest?

It's our job to beg down graces on these men: to preserve their vocations, to multiply the fruits of their labor, to strengthen their resolve, to call them to greatness. I recently heard a young priest thoughtfully answer the question *What do priests today need?* "We don't need comfort," he said. "We need *courage*."

In her excellent book *Praying for Priests*, Kathleen Beckman quotes Fr. John Hardon, S.J.:

> Having taught priests for over 30 years, having lived with priests, having labored for them, loving them and suffering with them—no words I can use would be too strong to state that the Catholic priesthood needs prayer and sacrifice as never before since Calvary.... But the pressures are experienced by priests with a violence and a virulence such as no one else but a priest can understand. One saint after another has declared that the devil's principal target on earth is the Catholic priest. Priests need, Lord, how they need, special

graces from God. We ask, why pray, then, for priests: We should pray for priests and bishops because this has been the practice of the Church since apostolic times. It's a matter of revealed truth. It is a divine mandate.[141]

So say an extra prayer for priests today: suffering priests, lonely priests, overwhelmed priests, the priest who baptized you, the priests who give you the Eucharist, the priest who prepared you for your first reconciliation and heard your confession ... Who knows? The connection may be so powerful it may reach all the way into eternity and shake you awake at night. God has a way of connecting us like that. He is a good Father.

Prayer for Priests

O Almighty and Eternal God, look upon the
Face of Thy Christ, and for love of Him Who is
the eternal High-priest, have pity on Thy priests.
Remember, O most compassionate God, that they
are but weak and frail human beings. Stir up in them
the grace of their vocation which is in them by the
imposition of the Bishop's hands. Keep them close
to Thee, lest the enemy prevail against them, so that
they may never do anything in the slightest degree
unworthy of their sublime vocation.
O Jesus, I pray Thee for Thy faithful and fervent
priests; for Thy unfaithful and tepid priests; for Thy
priests laboring at home or abroad in distant mission
fields; for Thy tempted priests; for Thy lonely and
desolate priests; for Thy young priests; for Thy aged

---

[141] Kathleen Beckman, *Praying for Priests: A Mission for the New Evangelization* (Manchester, NH: Sophia Institute Press, 2014), 20–21.

To Be an Apostle with You

priests; for Thy sick priests; for Thy dying priests;
for the souls of Thy priests in Purgatory.
But above all I commend to Thee the priests
dearest to me: the priest who baptized me; the
priests at whose Masses I assisted and who gave
me Thy Body and Blood in Holy Communion;
the priests who taught and instructed or helped
me and encouraged me; all the priests to whom I
am indebted in any other way, particularly (your
priest's name here). O Jesus, keep them all close to
Thy heart, and bless them abundantly in time and
in eternity. Amen. Mary, Queen of the clergy, pray
for us; obtain for us many and holy priests. Amen.

— Richard Cardinal Cushing

Questions for Reflection

Which priests have been most influential in your life?

Do you have a regular practice of prayer
for priests and seminarians?

How else can we support our priests?

30

Motherhood according to the Spirit

God has created each one us, every human being, for greater
things — to love and to be loved. But why did God make
some of us men and others women? Because a woman's love
is one image of the love of God, and a man's love is another
image of God's love. Both are created to love, but each in
a different way. Women and men complete each other and
together show forth God's love more fully than either can
do alone.

That special power of loving that belongs to a woman is
seen most clearly when she becomes a mother. Motherhood
is the gift of God to women. How grateful we must be to
God for this wonderful gift that brings such joy to the whole
world, women and men alike! Yet we can destroy this gift
of motherhood, especially by the evil of abortion, but also
by thinking that other things like jobs or positions are more
important than loving, than giving oneself to others. No
job, no plans, no possessions, no idea of "freedom" can take
the place of love. So anything that destroys God's gift of

motherhood destroys His most precious gift to women—the ability to love as a woman.[142]

So wrote Mother Teresa in a letter to the participants of the 1995 United Nations Conference on Women in Beijing. So simply, so clearly, so powerfully she stated what should perhaps be obvious but what has been obscured in an age of extreme confusion about the dignity of a woman's unique vocation: that a woman's motherhood is God's "most precious gift" to her because through it she loves in a way that mirrors His. It is a woman's superpower, this "special power of loving." It holds immense creative strength, and it is a great threat to the enemy's kingdom. Satan cannot create; he can only warp and distort. In his eternal frustration, envy, and rage, he seeks to destroy this incredible God-given gift to the world. He tries to convince women that their maternal nature, rather than something knit into their very being, is taught, something society writes like a fictional narrative, which is nothing more now than evolutionary baggage—and which can be tossed aside or stifled for the sake of other things.

And so God—in anticipation of the lies—raises up icons of Our Lady, of our Mother, in the bouquet of women saints and says, *Here—here is motherhood. Here are women who reflect beautifully this restorative, redemptive kind of love that gives life to the world.* And He heals our world through their supreme self-giving and makes the beauty of motherhood palpable, touchable, and able to be imitated in our lives.

---

[142] Mother Teresa of Calcutta, "Mother's Message for the World Conference on Women in Beijing," September 1995. A copy of the original can be viewed on "Mother Teresa's Message on Women," *Even the Sparrow* (blog), https://eventhesparrow.com/mother-teresas-message-on-women/.

Motherhood according to the Spirit

When I first read Mother Teresa's letter, quoted above, as a college student, I remember being struck by the woman behind the words — a woman who had given up natural motherhood for the sake of consecrated virginity but who became a spiritual mother to thousands dying in the slums of Calcutta and to all of us who learned from her how to love "the least of these." Mother Teresa pointed us back to the lost and lonely in our own homes. She urged us to not forget the unborn. She nudged us closer to Jesus and nourished the hesitant longing in our hearts for Him. She was, in every real sense of the word, a mother. She was completely and authentically a woman, and so really *she could be nothing else.*

Virginity according to the Gospel means renouncing marriage and thus physical motherhood. Nevertheless, the renunciation of this kind of motherhood, a renunciation that can involve great sacrifice for a woman, makes possible a different kind of motherhood: motherhood "according to the Spirit" (Rom. 8:4). For virginity does not deprive a woman of her prerogatives. Spiritual motherhood takes on many forms. In the lives of consecrated women, for example, who live according to the charism and the rules of the various apostolic institutes, it can express itself as concern for people, especially the most needy: the sick, the handicapped, the abandoned, orphans, the elderly, children, young people, the imprisoned and, in general, people on the edges of society. In this way, a consecrated woman finds her Spouse, different and the same in each and every person, according to His very words: "As you did it to one of the least of these my brethren, you did it to me" (Matt. 25:40). Spousal love always involves a special readiness to be poured out for the sake of those who come within one's range of activity. In marriage, this readiness, even though open to all, consists mainly in the love that parents give to their children. In virginity, this readiness is open to all people, who are embraced by the love of Christ the Spouse.

Spousal love—with its maternal potential hidden in the heart of the woman as a virginal bride—when joined to Christ, the Redeemer of each and every person, is also predisposed to being open to each and every person. This is confirmed in the religious communities of apostolic life, and in a different way in communities of contemplative life, or the cloister.[143]

Elizabeth fully lived her vocation as a bride of Christ. But she also embraced her feminine vocation as a spiritual mother. She did so in her tender concern for her own aching mother, her devotion to her sister, the attention in her letters to the sorrows and joys in those whom God had given her to love. She saw each person with an intuitive sensitivity; she saw right into their souls. She mourned with a friend who had lost her baby daughter, and she led her gently to Mary: "My heart," she said, "needs to tell you right away that it is one with yours and asks Him who inflicted the wound to heal it, for only He can do so! I understand so well the grief of your heart, my dear little Marie-Louise, that I won't try to bring you human consolation; you should take refuge in a Mother's heart, the heart of the Virgin. It knew all the breaking, all the tearing, and it always stayed so calm, so strong, for it always stayed leaning on the heart of Christ!"[144]

A woman's heart, a woman's soul, is created to be like Mary's—a refuge, a hiding place, a "shelter in which other souls may unfold," in the words of St. Edith Stein.[145] Elizabeth was that emotional

---

[143] Pope John Paul II, *Mulieris Dignitatem*, no. 21.
[144] Letter 134, in Nash, *Complete Works*, vol. 2, 61.
[145] Edith Stein, *Essays on Woman* (Washington, DC: ICS Publications, 2017), 132.

and spiritual shelter for everyone who knew her. When another friend mourned her husband, Elizabeth empathetically assured her, that "My whole soul, my whole heart are one with yours, for you know, Madame, what deep affection unites me to you."[146] When the Carmelite heard that her sister had a little Elizabeth of her own (baby "Sabeth" was born March 11, 1904), she admitted to crying "like a little baby."

> Oh, my Guite, I think I love this little angel as much as her little mama, and that's saying a lot. And then, you know, I feel completely filled with reverence before this little temple of the Holy Trinity; her soul seems like a crystal that radiates God, and if I were near her, I would kneel down to adore him who dwells within her. My Guite, would you kiss her for her Carmelite aunt, and then take my soul along with yours to recollect yourself close to your little Sabeth. If I were still with you, how I would love to cuddle her, to rock her … goodness knows what else! But the good God has called me to the mountain so I can be her angel and envelop her in prayer, and I very joyfully sacrifice everything else to Him for her sake; and then, there is no distance for my heart, and I am so close to you, you do feel that, don't you?[147]

From behind the walls of the convent, Elizabeth's maternal love had been transformed and enriched and taken on a new, deeper power. She pledged to nourish the spiritual life of her niece, and her prayers were not without effect: little Sabeth would eventually enter the same convent as her aunt!

Because she was so attentive to the spiritual growth of her sister, too, teaching Guite about the Trinity dwelling in her soul, she had

---

[146] Letter 195, in Nash, *Complete Works*, vol. 2, 150.
[147] Letter 196, in Nash, *Complete Works*, vol. 2, 151–152.

the holy audacity to claim that when Guite got to heaven, "I will rejoice to see my most beautiful Christ in your soul; I won't be jealous but with a mother's pride I will say to Him: It is I, poor wretch, who have brought forth this soul to your life."[148] When she became sick, she intuited that from heaven she felt that her maternal role would only grow stronger.

This was how she saw the Marian life of any Carmelite, "as a twofold vocation: 'virgin-mother.' Virgin: espoused in faith by Christ; mother: saving souls, increasing the number of the adopted children of the Father, the co-heirs of Jesus Christ."[149] She had an excellent model in her superior, Mother Germaine, who saw her beloved Elizabeth sensitively through spiritual darkness, relaxed rules when prudent for Elizabeth and her family, and stayed steadfastly by her side during her illness and death. "If you knew what a Mother I have at my side: a true mama, her heart has the tenderness, the delicacy known only to the hearts of mothers," she confided to a friend.[150] When Elizabeth was too sick to receive Communion, for example, Mother Germaine would lovingly come to kneel at her bedside after receiving the Eucharist each morning so that Elizabeth could adore the Lord, fully present within her. In her tenderness, she revealed to Elizabeth what every mother reveals: the very face of God, full of mercy and love.

The Church, a mother herself, invites each woman to embrace the receptive, intuitive, attentive, sensitive, reflective, and, especially, maternal love that is hers. The Church calls each woman to make a supreme gift of herself and to see souls come to life under the umbrella of her feminine heart, regardless of her state in life, her personality, her particular mission, or the brokenness of her past

---

[148] Letter 239, in Nash, *Complete Works*, vol. 2, 215.
[149] Letter 199, in Nash, *Complete Works*, vol. 2, 157.
[150] Letter 268, in Nash, *Complete Works*, vol. 2, 263.

or her current circumstances. The Church encourages each woman to participate in the redemption of the world and the restoration of all things to God under Christ and to do so with a particular spiritual beauty. And the Church needs both men and women to radiate the very love of God, in their own ways, as Mother Teresa said, "more fully than either can do alone."

Questions for Reflection

Who has had a maternal influence in your life?

Do you see the complementary nature
of the love of man and woman?

How does this reflect God to you?

31

Teach Us to Pray

When I was a little girl, my parents had a secret language they would use to converse about things in their private grown-up world. Well, actually, it was Spanish. Dad had been a Spanish teacher, and Mom knew enough to get by (and often it was just about whether there was ice cream in the freezer), but to us kids, it was totally foreign and their conversations felt frustratingly impenetrable.

Then I started high school, and I began to study Spanish myself. And word by word I began to make sense of my parents' "secret" language, learning sounds and accents, verb tenses and pronouns. As I became more comfortable, I could be drawn into their inner circle too. I was often clumsy with the language and got tangled in the words, but after several years, I would sometimes find myself thinking in Spanish.

This is similar to learning the language of prayer: the words of the Holy Spirit, the language of the Word Himself, the inner language of divine, Trinitarian love. It does not come at once but with a little practice and a lot of grace, we can find ourselves fluent in what is really our "mother tongue."

What is prayer?

The *Catechism* begins its section on prayer with a quote from St. Thérèse of Lisieux:

For me, prayer is a surge of the heart; it is a simple look turned toward heaven, it is a cry of recognition and of love, embracing both trial and joy. (2558)

Elizabeth would say, "Think that you are with Him, and act as you would with Someone you love; it's so simple, there is no need for beautiful thoughts, only an outpouring of your heart."[151] Foundational for true, deep prayer—the kind that Thérèse knew, the kind that St. Elizabeth knew—is the understanding that by virtue of our Baptism, God Himself is present in our souls. Pope St. John Paul II, in fact, said of St. Elizabeth that she was "a witness to the grace of baptism."[152] The journey into the depths of our hearts, the journey to Him waiting in the silence of our "inner garden": that is the journey of prayer. And mystical prayer, prayer of deep, intimate communion with God, is actually an ordinary—meaning for everyone—development of baptismal grace.

Prayer begins where it must begin: with words, learned as children or new Christians, recited and memorized: Our Fathers and Hail Marys and Acts of Contrition—made meaningful and internalized as they mark the beginnings of the path of total union with a Father who finds our fumbling childish efforts irresistible.

Prayer begins with the Bible, with the words of Christ, with an encounter with His promises and His reality and His love. It begins with a breaking open of the story that holds within it our salvation and with our yes to following Jesus into the story as it is played out in our lives. It begins with reading, reflecting on, and talking to God freely and tenderly and intimately about His holy mysteries and the new reality He is unveiling in our hearts—and, in so doing, moving—sometimes imperceptibly—closer and closer to Him.

---

[151] Letter 273, in Nash, *Complete Works*, vol. 2, 271.
[152] Mosley, *Elizabeth of the Trinity*, vol. 1, 407.

And then something shifts. Our souls become dissatisfied with the paleness of human words and sense a need for stillness, a need for quiet. If we surrender to it, prayer becomes a falling silent within an immensity of love, an awareness of being under the great and beautiful weight of God's gaze. We feel terribly inadequate to meet that gaze, aware of our smallness (our "abyss of nothingness," Elizabeth would call it) and the sheer wonder of being able to participate in the prayer of Christ Himself: a hymn of love to the Father, in the Spirit.

We find ourselves instinctively taking a posture of receptivity, of openness to a movement that renews and waters and rolls the soil of our "inner garden" into soft ground for grace to take hold and grow impossibly deep roots. And we realize that we now think more with the mind of God, and yet, as we feel our hearts expanding and ourselves becoming more human, we discover that we are becoming more fully ourselves — recovering the authentic, whole "self" God intended from the beginning when He first spoke us into being. The closer we get to God, the more we come home to ourselves — *habitare secum*, as St. Benedict called it: "to dwell with oneself."

The sure sign that this homecoming kind of prayer is having an effect on the soul is that it cascades out into life. It translates very naturally into love and virtue in the activity of our day, maybe without our even noticing. The fruit of the silence ripens into a peaceful living below the rush and noise of the modern world, of total openness and availability and being wholly present to the things of God, including His living image in the other souls we come in contact with.

Elizabeth had long been drawn to this kind of prayer. It was the charism that first attracted her to the Carmelite Order, and there in the convent, it had blossomed, transforming her more and more into a reflection of her Beloved. She habitually presented herself to God in a movement that was simple and pure. She lived for the liturgy and the hours of formal prayer her order was dedicated to, but when they were over, she was more inclined to set words aside and sit at God's feet—or bury herself in the Trinity, in the spirit of her religious name.

Discovering the spiritual masters of the Carmelite order only reinforced her inner experience. She wrote to her seminarian friend, full of enthusiasm after reading St. John of the Cross's *Spiritual Canticle*:

> To think that God calls us by our vocation to live in this holy light! What an adorable mystery of charity! I would like to respond to it by living on earth as the Blessed Virgin did, "keeping all those things in my heart," burying myself, so to speak, in the depths of my soul to lose myself in the Trinity who dwells in it in order to transform me into itself. Then my motto, my "luminous ideal," as you said, will be accomplished: it will really be Elizabeth of the Trinity![153]

After Elizabeth died, a folded piece of paper torn from a notebook was found tucked among her things. It revealed a treasure: an untitled prayer Elizabeth had written after a retreat given in November 1904. This eight-day retreat on the theme of the Incarnation was given by Fr. Fages, a Dominican, who spoke powerfully about the Holy Spirit. He invited the nuns to extend the mystery of the Annunciation into their lives by asking the Holy Spirit to come upon them: "Spirit of God, come upon me as you came upon the chaos of the world, as you came upon the Virgin Mary to create in her Our Lord."[154]

When we read her prayer to the Trinity, we don't doubt that Elizabeth had asked for the Holy Spirit's descent. We don't doubt she

---

[153] Letter 185, in Nash, *Complete Works*, vol. 2, 136.
[154] Mosley, *Elizabeth of the Trinity*, vol. 1, 351.

had an "upper room" experience, because her personal prayer gives us a breathtaking glimpse into the flowing, reciprocal love she experienced in her soul. She makes the life and prayer of Jesus her own; it is her deep desire for God to renew His mystery within her. She prays to be "lost" in the Trinity even amid the darkness of this life.

This prayer she had kept to herself, but she would spend her last years teaching others what she was learning in her life of listening to God. As an apostle of prayer, she was a gentle but insistent guide. She deeply wished to awaken the desire for God in others and draw them to discover what she had experienced: that the Trinity was within. The Trinity was waiting. Sensitive to each soul in her small sphere of influence, she always adapted her words to their specific vocations and circumstances. Yet underneath the message was the same: to seek and dwell in the presence of a God who makes our souls His paradise. "Live in His intimacy as you would live with One you love," she urged her mother,[155] and she helped her craft a simple practice of "three prayers, five minutes each,"[156] during each day as a way to begin to learn this intimacy. She advised a friend in the world: "The entire Trinity rests within us, this whole mystery that will be ours in Heaven: let this be your cloister." [157]

And who would have guessed—certainly not Elizabeth—that her private prayer would end up in the *Catechism of the Catholic Church*, the final words in its section on the Trinity. The *Catechism* reads: "The ultimate end of the whole divine economy is the entry of God's creatures into the perfect unity of the Blessed Trinity (cf. Jn 17:21–23). But even now we are called to be a dwelling for the Most Holy Trinity: 'If a man loves me,' says the Lord, 'he will keep

---

[155] Letter 170, in Nash, *Complete Works*, vol. 2, 113.
[156] Letter 273, in Nash, *Complete Works*, vol. 2, 271.
[157] Letter 172, in Nash, *Complete Works*, vol. 2, 116.

my word, and my Father will love him, and we will come to him, and make our home with him" (Jn 14:23) (260).

And then follows, remarkably, the opening paragraph of her now-famous prayer, making St. Elizabeth of the Trinity the only twentieth-century female mystic quoted in the *Catechism*:

> O my God, Trinity whom I adore, help me forget myself entirely so to establish myself in you, unmovable and peaceful as if my soul were already in eternity. May nothing be able to trouble my peace or make me leave you, O my unchanging God, but may each minute bring me more deeply into your mystery! Grant my soul peace. Make it your heaven, your beloved dwelling and the place of your rest. May I never abandon you there, but may I be there, whole and entire, completely vigilant in my faith, entirely adoring, and wholly given over to your creative action. (CCC 260)[158]

And so, if Elizabeth's calling could be summed up in a sentence, if I had to reduce her life's mission to a single phrase in the Gospel, a way her life truly became an "effusion" of the Eternal Word, I am certain it would be this:

Teach us to pray. (Luke 11:1)

---

[158] For a complete version of this prayer, see "St. Elizabeth's Prayer to the Trinity," *Even the Sparrow* (blog), https://eventhesparrow.com/st-elizabeths-prayer-to-the-trinity/.

Teach Us to Pray

Questions for Reflection

How did you learn how to pray?

Do you feel drawn to the quiet, simple prayer that Elizabeth loved?

Do you believe that you were created to experience that prayer?

32

Take Up and Read

The force and power of the word of God is so great
that it stands as the support and energy of the Church,
the strength of faith for her sons, the food for the soul,
the pure and everlasting source of spiritual life.

—Second Vatican Council, *Dei Verbum*, no. 21

As a freshman in college, I "accidentally" ended up in an advanced
Scripture class that underclassmen were not supposed to enroll in.
With God, of course, there are no accidents: I sat in the front row
of that first class, listening to the professor break open the Old
Testament, mesmerized as I realized within a few moments that
life might never be the same. A cradle Catholic, I had always—by
the grace of God—loved my Faith. But that day I realized how
little I knew about it. I began to see a story unfold, a story that
began in Genesis and continued in the Church and of which I was
an integral part. I saw salvation history, which, until then, I had
consumed only in bits and pieces. Now we were going to start from
the beginning. I wanted as much of that as I could get. Within a
few weeks, I switched majors from English to theology and never
looked back.

Even then, it would be years before Scripture reading became part of my daily morning routine, but that class was a bigger morning: a dawn of my desire truly to understand, through the Bible, what God has done, is doing, and will do.

Among Catholics now, there is a renewed interest in studying the Bible, a breaking open of the Word. Our Church is collectively on a sort of road to Emmaus. Many of us gather in Bible studies to dive deeply into particular books and passages—and simultaneously to stand back to gaze at the unfolding of a breathtaking story with Christ as the culmination. We feel our hearts burning within us like the disciples whose conversation with the Risen Christ opened their eyes for the first time to the fulfillment—in Him—of the passages they had memorized as children. This renewal is a sure sign of the continuing work of the Holy Spirit in the Church.

But in France at the turn of the century, that wasn't the case. Most people didn't have a Bible or even access to the entirety of Scripture. Elizabeth heard Scripture at Mass, she prayed with it in the Liturgy of Hours, she possessed a collection of passages from the New Testament, but she never had an opportunity for biblical exegesis or study. She never had what I had been given as a young student: a chance to start at the beginning and read my way through salvation history with commentaries and histories and wise professors. Still, what she lacked in access and resources she made up for with a sort of supernatural aptitude for getting to the heart of Scripture. She read reflectively, meditating on the words, making them her own, applying them and allowing herself to be transformed. She treasured the inspired writings, pondering them in her heart like Our Lady. And she had the best teacher: she had the Holy Spirit.

She led her own little Bible study, too, in a sense: she shared what God unpacked in her maturing soul with all of those who unfolded her letters and read Scripture-based wisdom such as this:

Do you remember that beautiful passage from the Gospel according to St. John where Our Lord says to Nicodemus: "Truly I say to you, if one is not born anew, one cannot see the kingdom of God"? Let us therefore renew ourselves in the interior of our soul, "let us strip off the old and clothe ourselves anew, in the image of Him who created him" (St. Paul). That is done gently and simply, by separating ourselves from all that is not God. Then the soul no longer has any fears or desires, its will is entirely lost in the will of God, and since this is what creates union, it can cry out: "I live no longer I, but Christ lives in me."[159]

This last phrase resonated with her deeply because she recognized it as exactly what was happening within her.

Elizabeth's words so naturally mingled with the words of St. John and St. Paul, it was as if there was an infusion of the fruit of their words—of the Word—into the fresh spring of God's grace that was her heart. She called herself a "little vase at the source, the Fountain of life, so that later I can communicate it to souls."[160] And that's exactly what she did; effortlessly she wove Scripture, and the depth of meaning in it, into her letters and, later, into her beautiful retreats. It was another way she was ahead of her time, or really, outside of time altogether. She lived totally in the intersection of linear time and the eternal now where God enters our world and works to restore everything to Himself under the headship of Christ, the Eternal Word.

In particular, she came to love St. Paul, who had become a sort of spiritual father to her and whose "beautiful letters" she admitted to "studying with much enjoyment."[161] She shared his words

---

[159] Letter 224, in Nash, *Complete Works*, vol. 2, 193.
[160] Letter 191, in Nash, *Complete Works*, vol. 2, 144.
[161] Letter 230, in Nash, *Complete Works*, vol. 2, 201.

freely and with the assurance of one who had experienced in her own soul everything he wrote. "I am going to give you my 'secret': think about this God who dwells within you, whose temple you are; St. Paul speaks like this and we can believe him," she wrote with a simple, endearing confidence.[162]

The real secret was that she could make accessible to others the mysteries of Scripture because, interiorly, she sat long hours listening at the feet of the same Christ who walked in the Gospels. She was the constant, receptive companion of the same Christ who had appeared to St. Paul. She deeply understood His voice in the sacred pages because she had heard it in the depths of her heart, in the hidden place she shared with Him.

The insight and illumination Elizabeth had about the sacred passages came directly from the intimacy she had with their divine Author. And it went both ways. Each passage allowed her to penetrate in her prayer a little more of the mysteries of the One she loved above all else, inviting her to know and love Him more and more.

St. Augustine, at the very threshold of his definitive conversion point, heard the heavenly voice of a child chant, "Take up and read, take up and read."[163] Through tears, he opened the Gospel, and his heart was transformed.

We have the same call today. "Take up and read," says Jesus, ready to move the mountains in our lives and the stones in our hearts. He is ready to be revealed personally and lovingly to us in the only words we have which are both milk and honey, human and divine—and alive.

Just a few months before she died, Elizabeth wrote:

[162] Letter 249, in Nash, *Complete Works*, vol. 2, 230.
[163] St. Augustine, *The Confessions*, chap. 12.

"His word," St. Paul says, "is living and active, and more penetrating than a two-edged sword: extending even to the division of soul and spirit, even of joints and marrow." It is His word then that will directly achieve the work of stripping in the soul; for it has this particular characteristic, that it effects and creates what it intends, provided however that the soul consents to let this be done.[164]

Reading the Bible really can be the starting point for a deeper relationship with Jesus Christ. We are called to know Him with the same intimacy Elizabeth had. A few minutes a day, early, when the sun is barely peering through the blinds—a cup of coffee and a journal and a passage from the daily Mass readings, hand-picked by the Church: this is how sanctity starts. This is the habit that invites holiness. This is how we "consent" to a conversation we will continue for life ... and beyond.

Questions for Reflection

Do you read the Bible regularly?

Why do you think it is important to study Scripture?

Which passages of the Bible have made
the deepest impression on your life?

------

[164] "Last Retreat," 154.

33

The One You Love Is Sick

The evening of my life has arrived, the
evening that precedes the eternal day.[165]

—St. Elizabeth of the Trinity

My dad's oldest brother was a beloved uncle, a hardworking me-
chanic, a heroic Catholic, and a devotee of St. Joseph. As I shared
before, he loved to take my siblings and me out for bike rides, hikes,
and all kinds of outdoor activities. As we took the side roads out
to the trails and forests, a tattered book about my uncle's favorite
saint bounced on the dashboard of his car, a constant reminder
to the rest of us how much St. Joseph was loved by Uncle Dick.

Years ago, at the end of a long, painful battle with stomach
cancer, my uncle lay dying. He had been unable to move for some
time, so my dad was startled to see him suddenly sit up. He pointed
to the foot of the bed, and his voice, long silenced by his sickness,
said clearly: "There's St. Joseph!"

Just in time to take him home. St. Joseph, you see, is the patron not only of workers—what my uncle loved him most for, I
think—but also of a happy death.

---

[165] Letter 315, in Nash, Complete Works, vol. 2, 334.

This Present Paradise

New Year's Day 1906. It was a Carmelite tradition to draw a patron saint for the year, and Elizabeth pulled out her slip of paper to see "St. Joseph." She was visibly moved. The community wondered at her reaction: "He is coming to fetch me," she said. "He is coming to take me away to the Father."[166]

And before the year was over, her prediction would come true.

Because she never drew attention to herself, no one had really noticed that Elizabeth's health had been deteriorating, but for months, she had been increasingly tired and struggled to fulfill her duties. She suffered from headaches and stomachaches, and then it became more obvious: Elizabeth was basically unable to eat. Around March 19, 1909 (St. Joseph's feast day!), she was moved to the convent infirmary, where she spent the final eight months of her life.

Elizabeth was suffering from Addison's disease, a disease of the adrenal glands which was relatively unheard of then and thus went undiagnosed. It didn't matter, though; at the time, there was no cure. All the community and the doctors could do was try to make her as comfortable as possible.

She was so weak that she was unable to walk for a while, until, through a prayer to St. Thérèse, her legs were miraculously strengthened and she was allowed to participate in community prayer and adoration from a narrow, second-floor window that overlooked the chapel. Other than that, and a visit every other week with her family in the infirmary parlor, she would spend the rest of her life in her new, simple room. On the walls hung a plain wooden cross and a painting of Our Lady, St. Mary Magdalene, and St. John at the foot of the Cross. Nearby was a statue of Our Lady of Lourdes, named by Elizabeth "Janua Coeli" (Gate of Heaven) and a tiny cupboard where she kept all of her writing. Elizabeth had

---

[166] Mosley, *Elizabeth of the Trinity*, vol. 1, 437.

special permission to write a letter a day during her long illness, and so many of the letters she left behind, as well as her spiritual masterpieces, were written in those last painful months.

She survived on minuscule amounts of chocolate, cheese, and ices, slowly starving to death. But really, she had already died, long before, not only to the world but to herself. Her life had been a long but thorough purgation, and in such a pure soul, the illness became an occasion of tremendous fruitfulness.

For someone of faith, sickness is never just sickness. Joined with Christ, it becomes *redemptive suffering*, which carries the additional spiritual weight of such words as cross, love, surrender, transformation, sanctification, union, and even joy.

"Life is a succession of sufferings,"[167] points out Elizabeth, and yet we are taught by the world to avoid suffering at all costs — even if the result is sin. The world encourages us to run from sacrifice, to hide from responsibility, to numb ourselves, entertaining ourselves into oblivion, and to end life before we can experience the painful but beautiful pressing weight of the cross.

And while she admitted that at times she was anguished and afraid, Elizabeth saw suffering as something precious, sweet, and to be savored in the achingly transparent way it revealed Christ to the soul. She did not pray for her suffering to end, only that she could bear it. She chose to embrace the cross and, yes, to find deep joy in it. In fact, she named her room in the infirmary "The Palace of Pain and Bliss."

How is that possible? It was the fruit of her life of prayer. In other words, a life of drawing near to Christ naturally culminates in willing conformity to His self-surrender on the Cross: "Love must end in sacrifice."[168] And ultimately, suffering is always sent

---

[167] Letter 252, in Mosley, *Elizabeth of the Trinity*, vol. 1, 235.
[168] Letter 291, in Mosley, *Elizabeth of the Trinity*, vol. 1, 294.

or allowed by God as a sign of His love. It's a paradox shrouded in mystery and one the world will never understand.

But the gift of faith allows us to see, as Elizabeth did, that suffering is two things.

First of all, it is *purifying*. It strips us of ourselves. "Oh, if you only knew how necessary suffering is so God's work can be done in the soul!"[169] Elizabeth begs us to understand. Christ gave our suffering power and meaning when He died on the Cross. United with His suffering (and that is absolutely the key), our suffering is stripped of its blackness and becomes instead our very salvation. A soul hollowed out — carved, scraped to the bottom — by suffering has immense capacity for grace, for God Himself to come flooding in and accomplish what we were created for: holiness, that is, likeness to Jesus.

And then it becomes *redemptive*, a participation in the saving work of Christ. What He accomplished on the Cross mysteriously lives on and continues in us by way of our union with Him. "Christ has in a sense opened his own redemptive suffering to all human suffering."[170]

When we open ourselves to the power of the cross (and Elizabeth did more than that: she saw the cross as the crown of her life), our suffering becomes a vehicle to offer to the world the salvific power of Christ. "He wants me to be another humanity for Him in which He can still suffer for the glory of His Father, to help the needs of His Church," Elizabeth said.[171] To be a "redemptrix" with her beloved Christ would be the sign and seal of His love.

If Elizabeth saw her life as a "prolongation of his humanity" (in her prayer to the Trinity) and sought to repeat with St. Paul: "It

---

[169] Letter 308, in Mosley, *Elizabeth of the Trinity*, vol. 1, 322.
[170] Pope John Paul II, Apostolic Letter *Salvifici Doloris* (February 11, 1984), no. 24.
[171] Letter 309, in Nash, *Complete Works*, vol. 2, 325.

is no longer I who live, but Christ who lives in me" (Gal. 2:20), it was natural that she would become a prolongation of the Passion. Christ on the Cross, living again in her: "In my flesh I complete what is lacking in Christ's afflictions for the sake of his body, that is, the church" (Col. 1:24).

It became her mission. In fact, she refused pain relief, not because it was wrong, but because she felt that suffering for the sake of the Church was the very "work" left for her to do — her apostolate of suffering. And she would do it to the full.

It is amazing and humbling, but it is the desire of God for all of us that we participate in the salvation of the world through our little crosses. God doesn't have to do it that way, but He chooses to implicate us in the work of redemption.

My children "help" me in the kitchen, splashing and spilling and stirring up a storm, causing a lot of mess but totally invested in the pancakes we create together. It would be easier, quicker — and *a lot cleaner* — to do it myself. But I know better than they do how important it is for them to be a part of the process. And the process of making a meal — or making a sacrificial offering, in the case of Elizabeth — is also making a relationship of love that has a breathtaking power.

The power of Christ crucified within the suffering person is unleashed upon the world when that soul unites his or her sufferings to those of Jesus.

Elizabeth's sickness and suffering progressed relentlessly, and in need of a mother's comfort, she began to carry her little statue of Mary with her wherever she went. Sometimes it was all anyone could see as she knelt in adoration, doubled over in pain.

As her illness intensified, she found tremendous consolation in the phrase from St. Angela de Foligno: "Where then did He dwell but in suffering?" To someone who was so focused on the indwelling of the Trinity, the idea of Christ literally living within suffering and our meeting Him there was incredibly moving. It marked a turning point in her final passion. Could she really be even more transformed by love? The answer is yes, when love is limitless.

Just weeks before she died, she wrote to her mother: "More and more I am drawn to suffering; this desire almost surpasses the one for Heaven, though that is very strong. Never has God made me understand so well that suffering is the greatest pledge of love He can give His creature, ... [St. Angela of Foligno] says that the sign by which we recognize that God is in us and His love possesses us is that we receive not only patiently but gratefully whatever wounds us and makes us suffer. To reach that state, we must contemplate God crucified by love, and that contemplation, if it is true, never fails to end in the love of suffering."[172]

As a surprise for Mother Germaine, Elizabeth created a little cardboard cutout of a fortress and named it the "Citadel of Suffering and Holy Recollection," the "Dwelling of Laudem Gloriae while waiting for the Father's House." The door to this little interior castle was closed, but Janua Coeli, Mary, the Gate of Heaven, stood guard outside. She wrote a poem on the fortress, which began with these words: "Where then did He dwell but in suffering?"

She had so often invited others to meet her in prayer; here was her "rendezvous" with Jesus, now a constant meeting at the Cross.

Still, Elizabeth was human, and at times temptation found a way into her fortress as the disease relentlessly consumed her from the inside out. "I'm suffering so much," she admitted to Mother Germaine, "that I now understand suicide," and she looked meaningfully at the second-story window near her bed. But she immediately reassured her spiritual mother, "God is there, and He protects me."[173]

---

[172] Letter 314, in Nash, *Complete Works*, vol. 2, 332.
[173] See Nash, *Complete Works*, vol. 2, 353, n. 2.

She found that there was a certain sweetness at the bottom of the cup and that she was mysteriously strengthened with each new demand, each new spoonful of pain, carefully measured out by the Father's hand. "I did not suspect that just such sweetness was hidden at the bottom of the chalice for the one who drank it to the dregs," she said.[174]

Of course, she was speaking of heavenly cups and probably dreaming of them too. Her tongue was shockingly red and inflamed, her insides burned, but as the end neared, she could not tolerate even a drop of water. On fire with thirst but unable to drink, she referred to suffering literally and figuratively as a "consuming fire."

"My Mother," she told the prioress, "it is very bad, but I believe the first thing I will do when I get to Heaven is drink."[175]

Questions for Reflection

What have been some of the greatest
sufferings of your life?

Have you been able to see or experience
sanctification and redemption in them?

For what intentions can you offer up your
sufferings—large or small—to God?

---

[174] Letter 313, in Nash, *Complete Works*, vol. 2, 330.
[175] Nash, *Complete Works*, vol. 2, 257.

)

34

On Retreat with the Praise of Glory

Have you ever waved goodbye to someone heading off to a mission or a pilgrimage and turned back into the house, baby on your hip, to face a pile of laundry on the couch and sticky breakfast dishes spread across the counter?

Have you rubbed your eyes over a keyboard or a spreadsheet, knots in your shoulders and in your stomach, and daydreamed of a thirty-day retreat? Although you'd settle for a weekend. Anything.

Or maybe you've stood in line at the supersize grocery store and wondered what it would be like to live in a hermitage, a convent, a cave even — anywhere quiet. Then, maybe, you'd hear God. Then, maybe, you could find peace. Then, maybe, you could taste a little of what Elizabeth seemed to be savoring in her quiet, her solitude, her recollection, even her suffering.

St. Elizabeth of the Trinity knows the burdens we carry. She knows our longing for God, the incessant internal noise of our worries and anxieties, and the constant stream of distractions that seem to frustrate our search for Him at every turn. And in the middle of the suffering of her final illness, thinking about all of those things, Elizabeth took out a black notebook and began to write.

She filled seventy pages with luminous reflections on themes that had been resonating in her prayer: the divine indwelling, remaining in God, the example of the Virgin Mary, and living our eternal destiny beginning even now. She divided her reflections into ten days, two reflections for each day, and designed a personal "retreat" for her sister. It would be something to remember her by and to use as a guide in her own spiritual journey as a mom and a wife whose life resembled very little the life in the cloistered convent where her sister had spent the last five years.

But while on the surface, Guite's life looked far different from her own, Elizabeth knew that holiness is for everyone, and no state in life excludes anyone from knowing the Lord with the intimacy she had come to enjoy. She wanted that so much for her sister. She wants that relationship of divine love for each of us. So she wrote with that in mind: that no one—*no one*—was created to exist outside of the love of the Holy Trinity.

Guite wouldn't find out about this retreat until the notebook was given to her by Mother Germaine two months after Elizabeth had died. Now, "Heaven in Faith," as it has come to be known (along with her equally magnificent "Last Retreat"), is a gift to the world.

It was the first thing I read of Elizabeth's writings. And as I said in the beginning, it struck me as the key to being a recollected mom. "Heaven in Faith" was the lane on the spiritual highway that smoothly merged "the Carmel and the kitchen" and "the cloister and the carpool." We are all, in the end, going in the same direction.

It is beyond the scope of this book to examine her last writings, worthy as they are, in great depth, analyzing each phrase and scrutinizing each source. But let's stand back and look at "Heaven in Faith" as a beautiful whole and a hopeful message for our world-weary hearts and consider some of her themes as they play out in our lives. Following is my attempt to summarize "Heaven in Faith."

Jesus Christ, from His communion of love in the Trinity, desires that we be where He is—even now, here on earth, in time, surrounded by crumbs and receipts and sticky notes. Elizabeth wants us, from the very beginning of the retreat, to know that our home is in God—and not just in some distant future or far-off place or only for a few stolen and fleeting moments but habitually, permanently, and deep in our own hearts. This is nothing less than the sharing in the very life of the Trinity—what we were baptized into, what our souls were shaped for.

The rediscovery of God in our "center" is an ever-deepening encounter of our "abyss" (Elizabeth loved that word and used it often) of emptiness and longing and the expanse of God's merciful love: where a "divine impact" takes place.[176] To facilitate that encounter, God has designed everything in life to give Himself to us.

"Each incident, each event, each suffering, as well as each joy, is a sacrament which gives God to (every soul)."[177] Each little summons from our state in life, our duties, and our personal mission is a revelation of God and His will in each precise moment of our lives. Nothing is meaningless.

But, Elizabeth reminds us, everything else—everything outside of God's will—must be renounced. We must be stripped of everything other than God, at least in spirit. All the things that once seemed so important have to be allowed to lose their tight-fisted grip on our hearts. We must be fully surrendered, our wills conformed completely with God's, and allow ourselves to be transformed to the point at which "the Father in bending attentively over me can recognize the image of His beloved Son in whom He has placed all His delight."[178]

There is a divine fire in our deepest center, a furnace of love that destroys our sin and purifies and renews us. It is nothing less

[176] "Heaven in Faith," 95.
[177] Ibid., 97.
[178] Ibid., 98.

than the Holy Spirit Himself, whom we find in our acts of pure faith when darkness conceals His secret, penetrating work in the soul.

Elizabeth draws from her reading of St. John of the Cross and continues: In the Holy Spirit, the soul finds itself absorbed in loving God "'even in its relations in the world', in the midst of life's cares it can rightly say: 'My only occupation is loving.'"[179] And as we continuously love God in the demand of each moment, we discover a God who is "continually coming."[180]

God comes, and His love so fills us that we love Him—and others—with His own love:

We forgive with His forgiveness.

We see with His eyes.

We think with His mind.

We feel with His Heart.

Each movement of love, each expression of grace and wisdom, is another visitation of Jesus to our hearts and a manifestation of His continual coming.

We are called to be receptive, then, to the gentle knock that invites us to open the doors of our hearts to a tired child, a sick parent, a frustrated co-worker, a burdened soul, a broken life. Just when we think we have nothing left to love with (because it is true: "He asks for more than we ourselves are capable of giving"[181]), we will find a swift surge from within that is more than us—that is God, in another coming. Every time He enters the soul, He exhales more of Himself with the same breath that first stirred our clay, and the soul expands to receive Him, ever capable of more self-gift and more of the sweet but sometimes heavy demands of love.

What if we don't feel this love?

---

[179] Ibid., 99.
[180] Ibid., 100.
[181] Ibid.

On Retreat with the Praise of Glory

Elizabeth speaks from experience: when God is silent, we go to Him by faith, a faith so powerful that it makes things present in our souls before we possess their fulfillment. In other words, to choose to believe is to possess God, to receive our inheritance even when He hides Himself in a darkness the soul can't understand. To hold all of heaven within us even when the shutters are closed and all we can see is a sliver of light and our own dust, floating in what feels like emptiness. "Faith gives us God."[182]

When we make an act of faith, says Elizabeth, we give God our blind but unshakable love.

We feel no consolation. We love Him.

We see no miracle. We love Him.

We receive no answer. We love Him.

We struggle and fall. We love Him.

The world may crumble around us and collapse back in on itself, and we will stand on the rubble and look into the sky *and love Him.*

And the accepting stillness, the quiet, assent of our heart — that is the sound of our love returning His love.

Here we come to a beautiful paradox. Our souls, stripped and tried and tested and surrendered, finally in the center of ourselves, encounter not only the God who chose us for Himself from the beginning but also the image we were designed to bear. We find the true meaning of what it is to be human. *We find ourselves.*

We walk this earth as living images, eternally drawn to the One who has impressed Himself upon us. When we find Him, there, in our center, our "little heaven,"[183] it is with a cry of recognition: *Here is God, and here am I, too — the true me, the redeemed me, the me He thought of from the beginning to reflect His glory in the shape of my particular soul.*

---

[182] Ibid., 101.
[183] Ibid., 108.

And every soul was created with this image, created to know God in the depths of the heart—every soul was created to be holy. The one who is "holiest" is not necessarily the one in the convent or the monastery, or even the papal palace, but the one who remains under His gaze and allows it to melt and mold the soul "like the seal on wax, like the stamp on its object."[184] This, Elizabeth reveals, is the object of the retreat: "to make us more like our adored Master,"[185] to become what we were destined for from the beginning.

To be like Christ is to embrace fully the will of the Father. Whatever He wants for us, we want, even if that means our own small crucifixions: "we will," resolves Elizabeth, "climb our calvary singing."[186]

Elizabeth reflects on the great mercy of God in the face of our sinfulness, on the humility of heart necessary to descend to the depths of our weakness, where God waits, ready to fill us with Himself. Then she reveals the woman whose humility was so perfect that she "remained so little, so recollected in God's presence, in the seclusion of the temple, that she drew down upon herself the delight of the Holy Trinity"; and so "the Father bending down to this beautiful creature, who was so unaware of her own beauty, willed that she be the Mother in time of Him whose Father He is in eternity."[187] God's imprint is so deep and perfect in Mary that she is the supreme example for all who seek to contemplate God in their innermost heart. In the mystical months before the birth of her Son, this was especially true: "It seems to me," ponders Elizabeth, "that the attitude of the Virgin during the months that elapsed between the Annunciation and the Nativity is the model

---

[184] Ibid., 104.
[185] Ibid., 106.
[186] Ibid., 107.
[187] Ibid., 110.

for interior souls, those whom God has chosen to live within, in the depths of the bottomless abyss."[188]

Then she makes a point about Mary that would have resonated with Guite, with her children on her lap and her husband coming home and the demands on her time and her strength and her love seemingly divided. She reminds us that Mary did not live in a convent but spent her life in the world, not only in prayer but in serving her family and her neighbors.

The Blessed Virgin "divinized" the most "trivial things," said Elizabeth.[189] Baking and weaving and sweeping and doing it all while utterly given over to God. Every little thing became a moment for His glory. Mary's prayer and recollection did not prevent her from dropping everything and hurrying to her expectant cousin but rather compelled her to do so; they urged her onward to greater and greater love, loving not just God but everything good and beautiful and true that He created. Prayer and action, in perfect union: this, I like to think, was her seamless garment.

The second reflection for the final day is particularly striking, as Elizabeth develops a theme that has become an important part of her spirituality. She has already shared with her sister in her letters that she discovered this passage from St. Paul, and in it, her deepest identity: "We who first hoped in Christ have been destined and appointed to live for the *praise of his glory*" (Eph. 1:12, emphasis added). She sees herself as not just living to praise God, but *being* a praise of glory, to the point that believes that "Laudem Gloriae" will be her name now and in heaven.

And not just for her: she wants Guite to share this identity; in fact, it is for all of us: "In Heaven" she says, "each soul is a praise

---

[188] Ibid.
[189] Ibid., 111.

of glory of the Father, the Word, and the Holy Spirit."[190] But this is her special charism, and so she has a particular grace to explain to the rest of us how "we correspond to our vocation and become perfect Praises of Glory of the Most Holy Trinity."[191]

Our life of praise to God is nothing less than a willed participation in what we've been created for, a claiming of our identity. Her reflection, then, is not so much a technique or a way to become something as an explanation of who we are, who we were created to be. "A praise of glory is a soul that lives in God, that loves Him with a pure and disinterested love," she says[192] — in other words, completely under the power of the Holy Spirit.

A praise of glory is "a soul of silence"[193] that lives under the noise of the world and is pulled close to the heart of Christ, listening to the sound of His symphonic love and ready to be played, to be touched and moved and vibrate under His hand. The string of suffering? That is to be prized above all: it makes the most beautiful music.

A praise of glory is a soul that gazes on God and reflects back to Him all goodness, all righteousness, all wholeness and purity. With a look, God gives all of Himself and in a burst of praise, the soul returns love for love. Finally, a praise of glory is always giving thanks to God and, in this way, begins the work she was created to do for all of eternity.

What is remarkable is that Elizabeth frames "praise" as *a way to exist.* We must *be* praise. What we do — love, serve, pray, heal, create, nurture, protect — all of these flow from *who* we are: living acts of worship. A praise of glory is someone in whom God is glorified continuously.

[190] Ibid.
[191] Ibid.
[192] Ibid., 112.
[193] Ibid.

On Retreat with the Praise of Glory

Elizabeth brings the retreat to a close, saying that in heaven her identity will be *Laudem Gloriae*. But she writes the words as if they are her new signature. If, as she believed, our heaven begins now, then her deepest identity, determined at the moment God thought of her, also begins now. Deeper than Elizabeth Catez, deeper than Sr. Marie Elizabeth of the Trinity, it was more than a name. It was a personal vocation.

And from down here, I sometimes imagine I can faintly hear her playing the eternal song:

Holy, holy, holy, is the Lord God Almighty,
who was and is and is to come! (Rev. 4:8)

Questions for Reflection

Have you ever had a powerful retreat experience?

In Elizabeth's retreat "Heaven in Faith,"
what most stands out to you?

How can you live as a "praise of glory"?

35

Humility and High Ideals

"Here comes Sabeth at last to sit down by her dearest Framboise and visit—with her pencil! I say pencil for the heart-to-heart communion was established long ago, and we are now as one."[194] So wrote Elizabeth to her young friend Françoise de Sourdon, affectionately called "Framboise" (Raspberry) who was nineteen at the time of Elizabeth's death.

Elizabeth had been a sort of spiritual mother to her for a long time, and they exchanged many letters during her five years in the convent. This letter would be one of her longest and come to be known as "The Greatness of Our Vocation": pages long, written over days and in a state of constant pain and exhaustion, addressing topics troubling Françoise's heart. Apparently, she had asked Elizabeth about overcoming her natural inclination to pride (not unlike the younger Elizabeth herself).

So Elizabeth, well aware that her death was near, settled in and took the opportunity to explore gently the beautiful interplay of humility and magnanimity, two virtues that may at first glance seem contradictory but necessarily need each other.

[194] "The Greatness of Our Vocation," in Kane, *Complete Works*, vol. 1, 124.

Humility comes from the Latin word *humilis*, meaning "low." It is to understand who we are before others, but most of all before God, to know our creatureliness and our total dependence on Him and our great need for His mercy. It is to know that we have done nothing to deserve the outpouring of God's grace in our lives, to be utterly amazed at the power and providence He shows us at every turn. It is to desire to be little because Christ Himself was humble: "Learn of me, because I am meek, and humble of heart" (Matt 11:29, Douay-Rheims). Elizabeth said to Françoise that "the humble person finds his greatest pleasure in life feeling his own weakness before God." [195]

To be *magnanimous* is to be greathearted, to be willing to take the harder route, to face danger, to do noble things, and to have high ideals. As a virtue, it is to do all of these things and more for the glory of God. Think of St. Teresa of Avila working tirelessly to reform the Carmelite Order and establish new convents or St. Ignatius having the vision and perseverance to found the Society of Jesus, or think of hidden saints who courageously embraced their own crucifixions and bravely climbed the mountain of holiness without looking back.

Elizabeth wanted for her friend what she wants for all of us: to know that humility allows us to move aside so that God can begin His great work in us: our transformation in Christ. When we are re-created in Him, our likeness to the divine restored, He is free to work in us, to move beyond the limitations of our nature and to enter the world in great and glorious ways through our yes. Humility *allows for* magnanimity.

Elizabeth desired to free us from thinking not that we are small but that we are capable only of small things. On our own, that is true, but *we are not alone.* We have the life of the Trinity within us. "My three," Elizabeth would say.

[195] Ibid.

Humility and High Ideals

Is it okay—is it humble—to desire the heights of holiness and to wish that God would use us to draw others up with us?

Goodness, *yes*.

After all, it was St. Thérèse who felt confident she would be a great saint—not because she was great but because God is. She in particular—and remember, Elizabeth was one of her first followers—was a living image of a union of virtues that might seem exclusive of each other. She synthesized them perfectly. She was humble but aspired to magnificent heights. Thérèse, was, however, certainly not the first Carmelite to do so.

Fr. Marie-Eugène, O.C.D., comments on the interplay of humility and magnanimity in his Carmelite classic *I Want to See God*:

> Great desires are the hallmark of the great soul. Great desires alone can inspire courage necessary to surmount the obstacles that beset its way. They are the wind that carries the soul high and far. To convince us, Saint Teresa (of Avila) gives us the testimony of her own experience:
>
>> We must have great confidence, for it is most important that we should not cramp our good desires, but should believe that, with God's help, if we make continual efforts to do so, so shall attain, though perhaps not at once, to that which many saints have reached through his favor. If they had never resolved to desire to attain this and to carry their desires continually into effect, they would never have risen to as high a state as they did. His Majesty desires and loves courageous souls if they have no confidence in themselves but walk in humility, and I have never seen any such person hanging back on this road, nor any soul that, under the guise of humility, acted like a coward, go as far in many years as the courageous soul can go in a few. (*Life*, XIII)

Fr. Marie-Eugène continues: "Great desires and humility can go hand in hand, answering for one another, and mutually benefitting themselves. Humility alone can sustain the great desires and keep them fixed on their goal amid the vicissitudes of the spiritual life. On the other hand, it would be a false humility that would induce the soul to renounce its great desires and become a victim to tepidity or mere respectable mediocrity."[196]

In other words, we are not aiming for purgatory, hoping to slip someday under the gate of heaven by the skin of our teeth. We were not created and redeemed and baptized into Christ to circle the drain and pray to make it out alive. Rather, we are all called to go far beyond what we in our ourselves are capable of and to live as if God lives and moves and breathes in us — *because He does*.

"I believe," writes Elizabeth, "we must live on the supernatural level, that is, we must never act 'naturally.' We must become aware that God dwells within us and do everything with Him, then we are never commonplace, even when performing the most ordinary tasks, for we do not live in those things, we go beyond them!"[197]

Of course, this isn't easy. The great battle in every human heart since the Fall has been our natural, overwhelming tendency to pride. Elizabeth knew this, and probably thinking of her own struggles, admitted that "pride is not something that is destroyed with one good blow of the sword!"[198] It takes a lifetime of daily deaths to self to sever the strong string that pride wraps around our souls to keep us fastened to ourselves and to keep us complacent and

[196] P. Marie-Eugéne, O.C.D., *I Want to See God* (Notre Dame, IN: Christian Classics, 1953), 179–181.
[197] "Greatness of Our Vocation," 127.
[198] Ibid., 124.

"commonplace" in the spiritual level. We must die to ourselves to live for God and to be open and available when He does call us to do great things for the kingdom.

And we should expect to be summoned. The call may be hidden, but it will always be great; it will always be salvific. In God's mind, to be small is only to remain captive to earthly things—and not least of all to that magnetic force that we seem to want everything to revolve around: ourselves. But once freed from self, we aren't limited by our own brokenness anymore.

The Holy Spirit has plans for us; we just need to open the door to Him. We have to open it wide with confidence and the anticipation that we are being called for a purpose. We have to believe that the measure of our call is undoubtedly higher than we are and then get out of the way enough for Christ to glorify the Father through our transparent souls.

The struggle is always to swat away not only pride but also the lying humility that the enemy of our souls feeds us in our lowest moments: *Who do you think you are, anyway?* he says. *You are nothing.* (This, by the way, he wouldn't bother saying if we really were not a threat to him, would he?)

The truth needs to be louder than the lies. Elizabeth's voice rises above the din of sin and says we must be aware of the greatness of the human soul in grace and that by Baptism, we've already been anointed for a mission. And we've been equipped for it. So, yes, we must be humble and know that without Christ, we really cannot bear any lasting fruit—but with Him, there will absolutely be basketfuls left over.

We need to safeguard this identity, to protect God's gifts and graces, to say no to anything less than living our personal vocation to holiness and the particular brand of love we bring to the world.

We are very dangerous to the enemy of our souls when we know exactly who we are. "We are his workmanship, created in Christ

Jesus for good works, which God prepared beforehand, that we should walk in them" (Eph. 2:10).

God has created me to do Him some definite service; He has committed some work to me which He has not committed to another. I have my mission—I may never know it in this life, but I shall be told it in the next.... I have a part in a great work; I am a link in a chain, a bond of connection between persons. He has not created me for naught. I shall do good, I shall do His work; I shall be an angel of peace, a preacher of truth in my own place, while not intending it, if I do but keep His commandments and serve Him in my calling.[199]

—St. John Henry Newman

Questions for Reflection

Do you struggle with pride?

Do you struggle with false humility
or feelings of worthlessness?

Do you believe that you are called
to sanctity and to greatness?

---

[199] Newman, *Prayers, Poems, Meditations*, 26.

36

To Light, to Love, to Life

Death from Addison's disease should normally have come in three months; Elizabeth's crucifixion lasted more than ten. She once said she thought she would "have a very long purgatory,"[200] and it must have often felt that she was living one on earth.

Nine days before her death, Elizabeth's pain and weakness worsened considerably. She was confined to her bed, barely able to see or speak, gradually starving to death.

Physically and spiritually she was breaking from the world with total inner freedom, waiting only for the Bridegroom to come for her, and ready to wait as long as necessary. She wanted His will even more than she wanted to see Him face-to-face.

Like a wise virgin, she kept her lamp lit. At times in the final week, there was no other interior light. All inner consolations were extinguished so that the final offering would be complete, and she could unite herself even to the anguished feelings of the abandonment of Jesus on the Cross. But she never lost her composure. In the supreme witness of her final, joyful suffering, she modeled what Pope St. John Paul II called a "superior gospel": the gospel of suffering. That is, thunderous witness to the unshakable truth of

[200] Letter 224, in Nash, *Complete Works*, vol. 2, 193.

Christ—whether we feel it or not—with just one thing: peaceful, joyful surrender in the face of unspeakable suffering.

To use a phrase she had picked up from St. Catherine of Siena, Elizabeth was being "distilled," drop by drop, for the Church she loved. This is how a life becomes not only an offering but a sacrifice to the point of *holocaust*, a sacrifice given completely, consumed as if by fire until nothing remains. In the end, Elizabeth became the smoke of incense in her great culminating act as a "praise of glory."

"When a great suffering or some very little suffering is offered to us, oh, let us think very quickly that 'this is our Hour,'" wrote Elizabeth, "the hour when we are going to prove our love for Him who has 'loved us exceedingly.'"[201] This was her hour, creeping toward a twilight, inching its way to the eternal day, which from all eternity has belonged wholly to God.

It seemed that in the last few days, the inner darkness lifted, and Elizabeth began to see glimpses of heavenly daylight in her dreams. The veil with her was evaporating, too. "I am going to light, to love, to life!" were the last, lyrical words she was heard to whisper.

On her final night on earth, Elizabeth began to gasp for breath. By morning, she was calm, but the nuns realized that she was about to leave them. They gathered around her bed to say the prayers for the dying. Elizabeth seemed, to Mother Germaine, fixated on something above their heads. And then peacefully, around 6:15 in the morning of November 9, 1906, she dissolved into the company of her "Three."

She had written not long before to her sister, "When the veil is lifted, how I will be to disappear into the secret of His Face, and that is where I will spend my eternity, in the bosom of the Trinity that was already my dwelling here below."[202]

[201] Letter 308, in Nash, *Complete Works*, vol. 2, 322.
[202] Letter 269, in Nash, *Complete Works*, vol. 2, 264.

To Light, to Love, to Life

"In peace she made the gift of her wounded life,"[203] Pope St. John Paul would say in the homily for the Mass of Beatification. *In peace she made the gift of her wounded life.*

Moments later, one of the extern sisters slipped out into the quiet, early-morning streets and made her way to Madame Catez's house. Elizabeth's mother must have known what the messenger's arrival meant, but can anyone be prepared to hear the news of her child's death?

The broken mother cried out in anguish, but she then remembered what Elizabeth had gently instructed her to say when the news would come, and so she knelt bravely and prayed: "My God, You gave her to me, You have taken her back from me, may Your Holy Name be blessed."

Grief and loss, all wrapped together as a part of life. We can't escape it, yet it was never part of God's original intent for us. We were not created to say goodbye. Death is the terrible result of sin, and we feel it so deeply and wrenchingly because it tears apart body and soul — both integral parts of our being and what makes us human.

But when we were baptized, we were incorporated into Christ's life, death, *and* His glorious resurrection. What is glory if not absolute triumph? Death defines us no more. It has no more power over us — only a temporary separation of body and soul and, for those who remain, the terrible, aching loss of what is visible.

Although unseen, our connectedness is only made greater. And in the instant of her death, what seemed to disappear — Elizabeth's life — was suddenly simply too real and too bright for human eyes to see.

It was important to Elizabeth that her friends remember the reality of the communion of saints. She would write about it repeatedly.

[203] Mosley, *Elizabeth of the Trinity*, vol. 1, 405.

This Present Paradise

"A Dieu, my dear Antoinette," she wrote to her friend, "when I am up above, will you let me help you, scold you even, if I see you are not giving everything to the Master? because I love you! I will protect your two dear treasures and will ask that you be granted everything needed to make them two beautiful souls, daughters of love! May He keep you wholly His, wholly faithful; in Him I will always be WHOLLY YOURS."[204]

Yes, Elizabeth, please help us from heaven — we have so much need of your friendship and the graces God has given you to share with us. We have much to be saved from, sorted out, strengthened in, and yes, even scolded for! Somehow we know this: that you are more present, more loving, more alive, more ours, *more Elizabeth* than you have ever been.

You will be very present to me there, and
my happiness will grow in interceding
for you whom I love so much.[205]

— St. Elizabeth of the Trinity

Questions for Reflection

What about Elizabeth's death moves you the most?

How do we become more ourselves
when we leave this earth?

[204] Letter 333, in Nash, *Complete Works*, vol. 2, 359.
[205] Letter 341, in Nash, *Complete Works*, vol. 2, 364.

37

Let Yourself Be Loved

"Your little praise of glory cannot sleep, she is suffering; but in her soul, although the anguish penetrates there too, she feels so much peace, and it is your visit that has brought this heavenly peace. Her little heart needs to tell you this, and in her tender gratitude she is praying and suffering unceasingly for you! Oh, help me to climb my Calvary; I feel the power of your priesthood over my soul so strongly, and I need you so much," wrote Elizabeth to her beloved prioress after a comforting visit in the infirmary.[206]

Mother Germaine was a gift straight from God to Elizabeth. She was one of those souls who come into our lives just when we need them, whose gifts seem tailor-made to our needs, whom God directly uses to love and care for us.

She was a gift to the entire convent, and to the Church, as a natural maternal leader who was re-elected as prioress a total of eight times. She upheld unwaveringly the ideals of the Carmelite Order, but had a tender heart and broke—or at least relaxed—many of the rules regarding limited letter writing and visits for Elizabeth and her friends and family. She sensitively realized the extraordinary distress of Elizabeth's mother and hoped to relieve it. She

[206] Letter 320, in Nash, *Complete Works*, vol. 2, 341.

intuitively understood that Elizabeth had a gift and a mission and needed to write more extensively to open the spiritual horizons of those in her life.

Mother Germaine helped Elizabeth to offer her entire life to the Lord—first in her vows and then in her suffering and death. She clasped Elizabeth's hands in her own and strengthened her in her most important and anguished moments.

In those final months, Elizabeth came to see Mother Germaine as exercising a sort of priestly ministry over her. (This is, of course, not in the ministerial sense, but in the context of the universal priesthood we were baptized into when we were conformed to Christ as priest, prophet, and king.) She was helping Elizabeth to make an offering of herself to God in her final agony—gentle hands lifting the little "host" up to her Trinity.

Elizabeth also came to see something else. She saw in her weary prioress a beloved daughter of the King who, for all her devotion and holiness and service to Him, needed to hear and internalize a most fundamental message: *you are loved.*

And so, sometime in those last days, she secretly wrote a letter that she would tuck away for Mother Germaine to find after her death. The prioress would treasure the contents of that small white envelope for the rest of her life. In it, Elizabeth expressed the love of God in an outpouring of her heart, in desperate pain but desiring not to waste any opportunity to leave behind a word or expression of love.

Written as the fruit of deep prayer, Elizabeth composed it as a message that she believed came from God Himself, issued as a gentle command.

My cherished Mother, my holy Priest, when you read these lines your little Praise of Glory will no longer be singing on earth, but will be living in Love's immense furnace; so you can believe her and listen to her as "the voice" of God. Cherished Mother, I would have liked to tell you all that you have been for me, but the hour is so serious, so solemn … and I don't want to delay over telling you things that I think lose something when trying to explain them in words. What your child is coming to do is to reveal to you what she feels, or, to be more exact; what her God, in the hours of profound recollection, of unifying contact, makes her understand.

"You are uncommonly loved," by that love of preference that the Master had here below for some and which brought them so far. He does not say to you as to Peter: "Do you love Me more than these?" Mother, listen to what He tells you: *"Let* yourself be loved more than these!" That is, without fearing that any obstacle will be a hindrance to it, for I am free to pour My love on whom I wish! *"Let* yourself be loved more than these" is your vocation.[207]

What a testament to Elizabeth's gift of empathy that while consumed with pain herself, she was still aware of Mother Germaine's struggles: her worries, her burdens, her feelings of vulnerability and unworthiness and inadequacy. Still a young woman, she carried the weight of the world, or at least the entire convent, on her shoulders during a particularly difficult and uncertain time. Elizabeth knew that God wanted to have a special, unique, and unrepeatable relationship with this woman who had given up everything to be His.

"Let yourself be loved," she repeated no less than six times in the letter. Elizabeth focused more on being loved, on

[207] Elizabeth of the Trinity, "Let Yourself Be Loved" in Kane, *Complete Works*, vol. 1, 179.

surrendering to God's purifying, refining, tender, merciful, trans-forming love — than on loving. For all of Mother Germaine's work and worry for the community, all He really wanted from her *was her*. Elizabeth, more than anyone, knew what waited for her spiritual mother in the prayer which was at the center of her call: a love unfathomable in its tenderness and mysterious mercy — a love that, once received, transforms us into who we are. Elizabeth ached for those in her life — for everyone, in her ever-expanding heart — to know how sought after and how "exceedingly" loved they are. Within that call to "let yourself be loved" is a message for all of us:

> *Let yourself be vulnerable. Let your walls down, your carefully constructed fortresses breached, your fiercely guarded heart laid bare. Let your wounds be touched, your fears revealed, your deepest desires, damaged dreams, and most daring hopes unveiled before the Bridegroom, who has the power to redeem, restore, and resurrect them. Drop your independence and the idea — which you clutch so tightly — that you can do anything to protect and save yourself. And let Him love you.*

Our universal vocation is to love. "Ask Him to make me live for love alone: this is my vocation," Elizabeth wrote,[208] but even more fundamentally, it is to *be loved*. Our primary vocation is to be loved by God. What a radically freeing idea. If we simply al-low God to love us, then we have done the most important work of our lives.

And we might not always feel loved, or worthy of being loved (for all our desperate, clinging, grasping, searching for it), but that is exactly where faith comes in. In "Heaven in Faith," Elizabeth pointed out to Guite that believing in God's love for us is "our

---

[208] Letter 172, in Nash, *Complete Works*, vol. 2, 116.

great act of faith, the way to repay our God love for love."[209] If we forget, one glance at a crucifix should serve to remind us.

Oh yes, we are greatly, infinitely, loved.

Questions for Reflection

Do you struggle with feelings of unworthiness?

Do you believe in God's love for you?

How can you allow yourself to be loved by God? Is there a closed-off place in your heart that needs to be opened to His love?

[209] "Heaven in Faith," 101.

38

We Have Our Heaven Within Us

"Mommy," my eight-year-old daughter asked, "guess which I am most excited for: First Confession, First Holy Communion, or Confirmation?" She waited expectantly for my answer. I looked at my little girl, who was about to receive all three sacraments that spring, with so much joy. "First Communion?" I had a hunch. "YES!" She danced around the room. "Because Jesus will be in me!"

Oh, my sweet, I wanted to say, *Jesus will be in you in a new and profoundly beautiful way — to consummate your Baptism in a mystery of union we can only begin to understand. But He is in you now, has always been in you with the Father and the Spirit, and delights in your innocent joy, the joy that spills out of your big brown eyes, windows into your interior heaven.* But the moment slipped away just like the girl who went skipping out of the room to continue cutting out paper dolls.

This is the core of Elizabeth's message. It certainly wasn't original to her: it is solidly scriptural, straight from the mouth of Christ: "If a man loves me, he will keep my word, and my Father will love him, and we will come to make our home with him" (John 14:23).

It is part of the cohesive continuum of Church teaching, as in the words of the great St. Teresa of Avila: "If we consider the

219

subject properly, sisters, we shall see that the soul of a just man is nothing else but a paradise, wherein the Lord takes His recreation. What a beautiful room then ought that to be, think you, in which a King so powerful, so wise, so pure, so full of every perfection, delights Himself? I know of nothing to which I can compare the great beauty of a soul, and its wonderful capacity."[210]

St. Elizabeth of the Trinity made this theology of our interior sanctuary eloquently and transparently her own. She, true to her name and her mission, placed a particular emphasis on the Trinity: "At every moment of the day and night the three Divine Persons are living within you.... You are never alone again!"[211]

She wanted us to understand that if union with God is our end, then heaven is not a destination but rather a completion, a perfection of a state of being. This blessed existence can and should begin in the here and now, anticipating, in her words, "the eternal present."[212] "Time," she would note, is simply "eternity begun and still in progress."[213] The soul that welcomes God, worships Him, and keeps company with Him in the interior temple knows in the pale morning light what will be known later in the full sun: the splendor of divine inheritance, the face of the Father. Thus, we can live in an "anticipated heaven"[214] which the Holy Spirit creates in us. We can live the life of heaven even now because "we possess our heaven within us."[215]

This is nothing less than the Christian understanding of hope. Union with God isn't something we hope *might* happen in some distant future, but something we have been promised — if we keep

---

[210] St. Teresa of Avila, *Interior Castle*, chap. 1.
[211] Letter 273, in Nash, *Complete Works*, vol. 2, 271.
[212] "Last Retreat," 162.
[213] "Heaven in Faith," 194.
[214] "Last Retreat," 151.
[215] Letter 122, in Nash, *Complete Works*, vol. 2, 51.

God's commands—and we look forward to in its fullness even while it begins in this very moment.

The purpose of our lives is not a remote future, but anticipated already now by faith. We begin to live our ultimate end—the union with the Trinity, even now in the secret center of our hearts where the Father, Son, and Holy Spirit begin to dwell at the moment of our Baptism.

In her short life, Elizabeth corresponded with six priests or seminarians, thirteen religious, and *forty laypeople*. This means that it was her particular mission to reveal that our state in life is only the external framework for the fundamental call to the heights of holiness that was knit together in our center long ago. In other words, we can all have heaven in our soul and live in the spirit of the cloister in our homes, in our high rises, and on our highways: "Whatever may be our way of life or the clothing we wear, each of us must be the holy one of God."[216]

Not unaware of the constraints and struggles of lay life, Elizabeth acknowledges a young mother's tiredness and the distraction of her daily duties but knows that what St. Catherine of Siena called the "inner cell" of her interior life was accessible to the busiest, weariest, and most distracted of all of us. This she knew not only in theory but also from experience in the years before she had been allowed to enter the convent. Her concern was that all souls know the interior Carmel she had discovered. This is remarkable because, in her time, there was less clarity in regard to the call to sanctity: priests and nuns were thought to dwell in a higher plane of holiness; laity had a lesser vocation.

In this respect, St. Elizabeth anticipated the Second Vatican Council decades before its documents underscored and articulated the universal call to holiness. She is something of a prophet of this

---

[216] "Heaven in Faith," 104.

great swelling of our understanding of the sanctity of the laity that continues to shape the Church today. She was fully a daughter of the Church, gifted by the Spirit with a unique charism to help bring about within the family of God a renewal of the interior life and the sanctification of the Church's members—all of them.

Elizabeth began her mission here on earth, but it continues even more fully from heaven.

The Carmelites in Dijon were among the first to have a devotion to St. Thérèse of Lisieux, so they were familiar with the Little Flower's declaration that she would spend her heaven doing good on earth. As she neared her own death, Elizabeth was asked if she would do the same. Elizabeth said that she would, instead, shoot "like a rocket" deeper into the abyss of the Trinity![217] But still, she had a feeling that there was more for her to do. Maybe it would be more of a hidden mission, but she conceded, "I think in heaven my mission will be to draw souls by helping them go out of themselves to cling to God by a wholly simple and loving movement, and to keep them in this great silence within that will allow God to communicate Himself to them and transform them into Himself."[218]

So whereas St. Thérèse has a knack for making herself known (how many roses has she tossed to us?), Elizabeth would work wonders while hidden in the heart of God and in so doing, draw us deeper into the love of the Trinity. When a friend left the convent and asked Elizabeth to pray for an outward sign that she would return, Elizabeth hesitated. "That is not my grace," she said.[219] The sign that Elizabeth leaves to show that she is with us is a *completely interior one*: that we find ourselves in a communion of love that we never thought we'd find.

---

[217] Mosley, *Elizabeth of the Trinity*, vol. 2, 194.
[218] Letter 335, in Nash, *Complete Works*, vol. 2, 360.
[219] Letter 293, in Nash, *Complete Works*, vol. 2, 297.

We Have Our Heaven Within Us

I believe that God honored Elizabeth's desire to be hidden for a long time as the cause for her canonization crept slowly forward. Finally, she was beatified by Pope St. John Paul II on November 25, 1984. The saint who preferred to be buried in the Trinity was brought out and presented to the Church as "a brilliant witness to the joy of being rooted and grounded in love," reflected the pope on that day.[220] He said that her teaching on the mystical life of the soul was spreading "with a prophetic force."[221] Her feast day was declared to be on November 8 (the day of her death, November 9, was already celebrated as the feast of the Dedication of St. John Lateran Basilica in Rome). It took three more decades for Elizabeth to be declared a saint, canonized by Pope Francis on October 16, 2016.

It was, at last, time to let her particular light shine in our inner darknesses, to reveal the God who waits within our souls, and to usher in a new age of the Spirit—a hidden movement of souls plunging deep into their interiority and transforming the Church and the world from the inside out. Of that I am convinced, and I am convinced that you are reading this now because you are a part of that transformation. Let's let Elizabeth lead us back to the temple of our souls, dedicated at our Baptism, and hold up a lamp in that consecrated place to show off the treasures within.

Show us, St. Elizabeth, that we do *have everything*.

We have our heaven within us, *let's live it.*[222]

—St. Elizabeth of the Trinity

---

[220] Mosley, *Elizabeth of the Trinity*, vol. 2, 403.
[221] Ibid., 404.
[222] Letter 120, in Nash, *Complete Works*, vol. 2, 49.

Questions for Reflection

What stands out the most to you from the life and writings of St. Elizabeth of the Trinity?

Do you feel that journeying with her has helped you grow closer to God?

Can you believe and embrace that you are called to be part of the spiritual renewal of the Church?

About the Author

Originally from Wisconsin, Claire Dwyer received a degree in theology from Franciscan University of Steubenville and now lives in the Southwest with her husband and six children. She received a certification in spiritual theology from the Avila Institute and works for the Avila Foundation as writer and editor of the website SpiritualDirection.com. Claire has contributed to CatholicMom.com, Women of Grace, Endow, the *National Catholic Register*, and the *Catechetical Review*. She speaks to groups large and small on topics such as authentic femininity, pro-life saints, and keeping space for the sacred in our lives.

She would love to stay in touch with readers through her blog, *Even the Sparrow*, where she posts regularly on everything from the saints to the spiritual life and the sacramentality of the everyday.

Her passion is to help fellow followers of Christ see the beauty and possibility of their interior lives and their unrepeatable place in His Church.

Sophia Institute

Sophia Institute is a nonprofit institution that seeks to nurture the spiritual, moral, and cultural life of souls and to spread the Gospel of Christ in conformity with the authentic teachings of the Roman Catholic Church.

Sophia Institute Press fulfills this mission by offering translations, reprints, and new publications that afford readers a rich source of the enduring wisdom of mankind.

Sophia Institute also operates the popular online resource CatholicExchange.com. *Catholic Exchange* provides world news from a Catholic perspective as well as daily devotionals and articles that will help readers to grow in holiness and live a life consistent with the teachings of the Church.

In 2013, Sophia Institute launched Sophia Institute for Teachers to renew and rebuild Catholic culture through service to Catholic education. With the goal of nurturing the spiritual, moral, and cultural life of souls, and an abiding respect for the role and work of teachers, we strive to provide materials and programs that are at once enlightening to the mind and ennobling to the heart; faithful and complete, as well as useful and practical.

Sophia Institute gratefully recognizes the Solidarity Association for preserving and encouraging the growth of our apostolate over the course of many years. Without their generous and timely support, this book would not be in your hands.

www.SophiaInstitute.com
www.CatholicExchange.com
www.SophiaInstituteforTeachers.org